W9-DDX-167

LEPERS

How Society's Outcasts are

NO

Healed and Restored

MORE

STEPHEN E. CANUP

with contributions by Brandon Hill,
Duane Brecheisen and Russell Stewart

Special thanks to Rev. Don Castleberry,
Founder, Freedom in Jesus Prison Ministries

Published by:
Freedom in Jesus Prison Ministries
www.fijm.org | info@fijm.org

Acknowledgements

Everyone needs a mature spiritual mentor and trusted accountability partner. I love and appreciate Don Castleberry for fulfilling this role for me. His trust, time and commitment to me have been invaluable. He has become one of my very best friends.

Rev. Don Castleberry is the Founder of Freedom in Jesus Prison Ministries. Learn more about this anointed prison ministry at *www.fijm.org* or, write to Freedom in Jesus Prison Ministries, P.O. Box 939, Levelland, TX 79336. You may e-mail us at *info@fijm.org*

Special thanks to Kevin Williamson for cover creation, layout and design assistance. For inquiries about his work, contact Kevin at *kevin@kevinwilliamsondesign.com*

Appreciation is also expressed for printing and shipping services through Perfection Press. For information contact Robert Riggs, *rriggs@printedtoperfection.com*

Table of Contents

INTRODUCTION

E X-CONVICTS IN GENERAL, and former sex offenders in particular, are treated as outcasts in modern society. Once a person is assigned a label of "ex-convict", "felon", or "sex offender", they are set up for many unique lifetime challenges and trials other people typically do not endure.

Internally, they are burdened with guilt and shame over their past, and are often hopeless to think anything good could ever come of their lives. Externally, they are treated by the world as if they were "less than", "separated", "unclean", "damaged goods", and "disfigured". People often become fearful in their presence, and assume that they can't or won't ever change. In a remarkably striking sense, they might be considered as modern day "lepers".

Many of us first heard of lepers, and leprosy as a disease, from reading the Bible or hearing Bible stories as children. In Biblical days, once a person was diagnosed as having leprosy they had to keep their head shaved and their clothes torn. They were considered "outcasts" from society. The Hebrew custom of tearing one's clothing was an expression of extraordinary emotion, usually of grief, terror, or horror. The tearing of one's clothes was also an expression of anger or despair. Among the people, they had to maintain a distance and constantly cry out, "unclean"!

"Leprosy was the scourge of the ancient world. Nothing evoked more fear, more dread, or more revulsion than the sight of these walking dead. That is what a leper was called, a walking dead man. The smell of his decaying flesh would announce his coming long before the tattered scraps of his clothing would be seen, or his raspy "Unclean! Unclean!" announcement he was required to declare, could be heard. The stumbling shuffle of toeless feet, the wandering of sightless eyes and the moan of a cheekless mouth, all pointed to Leprosy, this unseen attacker that slowly destroyed human bodies, and made the individual an untouchable to society."

(from Christianity.com as of 5/4/21)

In contrast to the rest of society, Jesus was neither repulsed by, nor fearful of, lepers in His time of ministry here on Earth. He allowed them into His close Presence; and, listened to, touched, healed, blessed and loved them. Jesus is still seeking and saving the lost, even those of us who are labeled felons, ex-convicts or sex offenders – modern day "lepers".

Of course, He is also seeking and saving those who have never been incarcerated–addicts, liars, cowards, gossipers, adulterers, idolaters, thieves, drunkards, swindlers; as well as the immoral, proud and covetous. Jesus loves us all, and wants us to choose to follow Him, and fall forever in love with Him.

God the Father sent Jesus to willingly give up his life, paying the ultimate price for all our sin for all time. To those who truly repent, receive Him, believe Him and confess Him, the resurrected and living Christ gives us His Holy Spirit to live in us! Christ in us and us in Him! As we truly surrender our lives to Jesus as Lord, and submit to the Leadership of the Holy Spirit, He takes away our guilt, shame and regret over our past. We are set free from the curse of society's labels. ***Truly, we are lepers no more!***

How can all this be real in your life? Let's find out...

FOUR TRUE STORIES
OF FORMER LEPERS

SPIRALING DOWN TO DEPRAVITY

By Stephen Canup

O utwardly, in the world's eyes, I was at the top of the ladder of success, the pinnacle of prosperity, and living the dream. With an office on Park Avenue in New York City, and making nearly $250,000 a year in 1985, I had it made. However, the hidden person deep inside me had begun to delve into an entirely different life style which would later lead to the very depths of depravity, perversion and reprobation.

Part of my destruction was revealed in my previously published personal testimony contained in my first book, *Jail-House Religion*, which now also appears later in this book, "From Park Avenue... to Park Bench... to Prison." Today, I am able to fill in some of the sordid details for the purpose of bringing more glory to God believing that more personal transparency will bring increased hope and freedom to others if they too turn their lives totally over to Jesus Christ as Lord and Savior. If God can change me, and He has, He can change anybody!

Having risen close to the very top of the business world as a Certified Public Accountant with the world's largest accounting firm, I maintained an outward persona necessary to achieve. However, my darkest inner secrets of twisted thinking and behavior were well hidden for a time, and I deceived my very own self–destroying my career, my family and my morals by descending into an ever deepening pit of darkness.

Although I was raised in a Christian home, I was exposed to pornography through childhood friends around age 10. Earlier, at age 6 or so, an older boy was in the woods with me behind my house, and in the process of committing sodomy with me, when my mother's voice rang out from the back door that supper was ready, interrupting him and saving me from his designs.

Both of these events introduced darkness in my soul at a young age giving the enemy a foothold he would use on and off for nearly fifty years to lead me into a secret life beginning with lustful imagination and self-gratification, eventually immersing me in triple XXX theatres and bookstores, and sexual immorality of every kind.

Since being saved in prison at age 57, I praise God that He has delivered me from darkness and from deep bondage to a prior lifestyle of sin, depravity and sexual perversion. Among the many addictions I once had, it was pornography, drugs and alcohol that fueled an immoral lifestyle. This was heightened by the fact that I never consistently took the psych meds prescribed for the bipolar diagnosis I received in 1989 at age 37.

It was as if there was a big, black pit in my soul that constantly demanded chemical and sexual indulgences; but it was never filled or satisfied in spite of everything I tried. Over the twenty years between Park Avenue and Prison, I was empty, bored, searching, seeking and restless. I felt powerless to resist almost every enticement presented me. Although I was once very ashamed of the behaviors to which I was led, I am forever grateful to Jesus Christ for finding me and setting me forever free (see Romans 6:16-23).

Where did it all lead? Without details, here are some of the things I struggled with or participated in over the years before I was saved: bisexual encounters, gender confusion, illicit hook-ups with strangers of both sexes, activities in back rooms of adult bookstores, gay bars, indecent exposure, and compulsive self-gratification. The shame and guilt I felt as a result of this lifestyle contributed to constant hopelessness, depression and several suicide attempts.

Jesus took all my shame so that I could have His righteousness; He took all my rejection upon Himself at Calvary so that I could have His acceptance by the Father. The saving work of Jesus, the love of the Father, and the power of the Holy Spirit are the only things that filled that deep pit inside me. The peace, joy, wholeness and abundance I have in place of the former black hole of emptiness is impossible to adequately describe; and, I am humbly grateful daily now that I am forever free of the condemnation, torment, guilt, embarrassment, shame, perversion and depravity that dominated my soul and life before I was born again. I am a totally new man in Christ Jesus (2 Corinthians 5:17-21). Praise God!!!

I will say it again, if God can save, deliver, heal and change me; He can save, deliver, heal and change anyone! I have learned to take the wrong kind of thoughts captive quickly so that I do not give in to the almost daily temptations the devil brings (2 Corinthians 10:4-5).

But before I was saved, I fell a mighty long way. I was unemployed for seven years, and homeless for three years, leading up to being sent to prison for the first (and last) time at age 56. My crime was solicitation of a minor and I thought my life would be forever ruined because of the label I now carried of "sex offender". I was sent to a medium security, medium term facility managed by CCA (now CoreCivic) in Nashville, TN, to serve my time.

At Davidson County Jail, before I was sent to prison, I requested something to read and the Chaplain sent me a pocket-size Gideon's New Testament. Reading was something I did often to "escape" when I was homeless, helpless and hopeless. Until I finally was able to go to the prison library, the Bible was the only thing I had to read. Since I had already heard men being made fun of for reading their Bible or going to chapel classes or services, I read mine out of the way of others while on my bunk, both in jail, and later in prison.

For the first ten or twelve months in prison, I stayed pretty much to myself and experienced a lot of fairly severe depression. I was not given any meds for bipolar illness so I was essentially stuck in the manic-depressive phase. No one knew where I was so I had no money on my books and did not receive any visits or letters. Sometimes I got out of my depression and despair enough to play some cards or dominos or watch television, but most of the time I was a loner. I kept reading my Bible a little late at night and in the early morning, but I primarily read spy novels, murder mysteries, and westerns. I did not attend chapel. My time drug by.

As I read my Bible more, I remembered what I had learned growing up in the Baptist church about Jesus forgiving all my sins and that He has a plan for everyone's lives. I had a very hard time believing that still applied to me based on all I had done and how far I had fallen, but I could sense a small glimmer of hope. Could God really accept me, forgive me, and love me? The Bible made it clear that He could and does!

Certainly I blamed myself for where I ended up and for the charges I had. I hated myself and could not bear to look into the mirror when shaving or brushing my teeth. I was overcome with guilt, shame, regret and embarrassment. I began to understood that God forgave me, but I couldn't forgive myself. I thought my past was so bad that I had no future.

In my addictions and sin, I had pushed away every family member and friend. My family didn't even know where I was nor if I was even alive. I had not tried to contact them in five or six years. The fact that I had always been so prideful made it impossible for me to reach out to them while I was homeless and unemployed. Now I was in prison where none of my family had ever been.

A major breakthrough began in February, 2009, when I felt God encouraging me to reach out to and ask forgiveness from my family. Humbling myself enough to write that first letter was so very hard, but I felt a huge burden begin to lift as soon as I mailed it. In a short time, I heard from my two older brothers. They said they weren't holding anything against me and both wanted to know what they could do to help me. Wow, what a miracle!

Then the Lord impressed in my spirit that if my family could forgive me, and He could forgive me, then I needed to forgive myself. Oh my goodness, what a sense of freedom from bondage began to grow in me as I decided to put my past in the past, forgive myself, and trust God with my future one day at a time. I reveal much more about this part of my "awakening" in my longer testimony, "From Park Avenue... to Park Bench... to Prison" later in this book.

I began to have more of a hunger for the Word and much less desire for the all the other books I was using as a means of mental escape to avoid dealing with my feelings and situation. On my 57th birthday, April 20, 2009, I attended my first Chaplaincy class that would last three months. I declare this date as my official "re-birth" date! Being "born again" is the very best thing that has ever happened to me. If it took going to prison to get my attention, so be it.

Soon after, I started going to Chapel when they called out for "church". People were surprised and made fun of me but I didn't care. I was being progressively filled with hope little by little. Having been absolutely hopeless for years, and in suicidal depression for so long, this was a very welcome feeling. Then I learned from Jeremiah 29:11-14 that God really did have a plan and a future for me. Yes, even me, a sex offender!

I went "all in" for Jesus. I have never looked back and I have never regretted my commitment, not even for a minute. I began to do every Bible Correspondence course I could get my hands on. I started a Bible study and prayer group in my housing area. For me, "Jail-house Religion" was "the real thing". Later in this book is an article I wrote with that very title.

My two brothers committed to help me get back to Texas as soon as I discharged my sentence. One of them knew the founder of Freedom in Jesus Prison Ministries, Don Castleberry, who began to correspond with me prior to release. Because I felt God had a call on my life for prison ministry, I moved to Levelland, TX, where Don lived and started volunteering in his ministry. He then agreed to mentor me and we were accountability partners. We spent a lot of quality time together and we have become best friends. As of Fall, 2020, I have the privilege of serving as President of Freedom in Jesus Prison Ministries, after having been Executive Director for about four years.

After a year under Don Castleberry's supervision, in 2012 I asked him to ordain and license me into the Gospel ministry. In prison, I made the commitment to serve God with all of my heart for all of my days. So on February 23, 2012, in front of fifty or so friends and family members, I publically submitted myself to a higher standard of lifetime accountability to God and the Body of Christ as an ordained minister and a licensed teacher of the Word.

My purpose and passion is to share the love and hope of the Gospel of Jesus Christ with every prisoner and inmate I can. My longer testimony later in this book is provided to share many of the concepts, principles and truth I learned while in prison, and then extending in the free world since I was released December 29, 2010. I pray you will read it all and be encouraged.

I will say it again, if God can change me (and He surely has), He can change anyone who will surrender their lives, seek Him with all their heart, and be willing to follow hard after Jesus!

THERE IS STILL HOPE AND LIFE AHEAD

By Brandon Hill

It gives me great pleasure to share with you how God has redeemed me and given me a new life. To share a little bit about my past, I was raised in a single-parent home with only my little brother and my mother. We were very poor growing up. My mother was a very hard-working woman who was very loving and always encouraged us to do the right things. She would take us to church often and even pray with us at night before bed. In spite of my mother's attempt to raise my brother and myself in the right way, our away from home environment and the people in it was the total opposite.

Once I reached my early teens my mother's work schedule changed leaving my younger brother and I with a lot of time to ourselves. That is when I began running the streets and became associated with the gang life. From there my life became full of violence and chaos. This lifestyle led me into two felonies. My first charges were aggravated assault with a deadly weapon, for a drive-by shooting; and then a deadly conduct charge I received while out on bond on the first charge. Surprisingly, I ended up receiving 10 years adjudicated deferred probation for both charges.

Unfortunately, it didn't take long before I violated my probation. By God's grace I was sentenced to two 5-year sentences running concurrently. I ended up doing 4 years and 1 month on the sentence. So, I was left with only 11 months to do on parole. Once I was released, I was determined to stay out of trouble and to never return to that lifestyle again.

The first day I was released a so-called "friend" offered me drugs knowing I had to report to parole the next day. I quickly declined the drugs knowing the seriousness of my decision. Temptation came to me in every form possible within my first month of being released. Things were tougher upon my release than they otherwise would have been because I decided to return to the same old environment around the same people as before.

The strength and fortitude of my decision to never return to my old life style was challenged on all levels. Slowly my resolve was wearing down and my decisions became full of compromise leading me into a lot of high-risk situations and surrounding myself again with the types of people I vowed to stay away from. I never became associated with the gangs again, but instead traded that lifestyle in for the party lifestyle thinking that was a better alternative.

Eventually, my life became consumed with drinking, clubbing, and chasing women. This was a trick of the devil, and I fell into the deception of thinking that the trading in of one type of destructive lifestyle for another was more acceptable. This led me to making the mistake of sleeping with a woman whom the courts deemed too intoxicated to legally consent. Once I knew about the charge of sexual-assault being filed on me, I eventually turned myself in, went to trial and received a 21-year sentence.

At one point during my incarceration I was close to being released and the charges dropped, so words could not express how angry I was over the whole thing once I was sentenced. I felt like I had fallen into a dark bottomless pit with no hope of ever getting out. My anger was towards everyone around me, including both myself and God. I felt so alone and lost. Confused about how I had allowed my life to get to this point, I was full of shame and disappointment from letting my children and family down. All of these negative and mixed-up emotions took me into a dark place and foolish mind-set.

I had convinced myself at one point that I had to forget about having a normal life ever again, and also just to forget about the free world. There was no hope left inside. Eventually, I turned to drugs, alcohol, and gambling while incarcerated to numb my pain and to remove my mind from focusing on the debilitating shame and disappointment I had inside. This type of negative behavior went on for almost 10 years.

Coincidentally, both my mom and dad, who had been divorced since I was three years old and separated, both had been diagnosed with cancer while I was incarcerated. This took a great toll on me especially with my mom because she was the only person that had always been there for me. It broke my heart not being able to support her while she went through it. Regarding my dad, he and I had just really begun to mend our broken relationship after all these years and then this happened. I remember getting the news of my mom's diagnosis over the phone trying to fight the tears not wanting anyone to see me crying. I went to my bunk and cried for the first time in a long time and said a prayer for my mom–something I had not done in years. Fortunately, my mom was healed miraculously by God.

My dad on the other hand passed away from cancer. His death triggered something inside of me that motivated me to make some positive changes in my life. Slowly I began to pull away from drugs and drinking that had caused me to be numb to all of my many issues. While still in prison I made up my mind to enroll and complete college to honor my dad. Right after my father's passing, I signed up for the Kairos spiritual retreat weekend in my facility. At the time I had no way of knowing that God was going to use that program and those four days to transform my life forever.

When I attended Kairos, everything shifted in my life. The Presence and Love of God was so strong in that place that you could feel it in the air. The last day of the program after the forgiveness ceremony my heart was completely broken and open to God. I remember feeling so light after the forgiveness ceremony that I looked down four times just to make sure my feet were still on the ground. It was then that I made up my mind to spend the rest of my life serving God.

After that Kairos weekend I spent almost all of my time reading the Word of God. Slowly the Holy Spirit started opening my eyes to my many issues and how to deal with them. This was a very hard process that God took me through, but He got me through it in a victorious way. As God began to change me, things began to change for me. I was moved into the Faith Based Dorm unawares. I never signed up for it so the fact that it happened I took as a sign from God.

Being there turned out to be one of God's biggest blessings to me. God used that place to cultivate and nurture my faith and relationship with

Him. God opened up several doors and surprisingly, I was asked to be one of the twelve mentors in the Faith Based Dorm. It was truly a blessing to be used by God to help others. Soon after, I was asked by the Chaplain to be the Faith Based Dorm Coordinator, which I accepted. God also opened the door for me to learn how to play the drums and it wasn't long before I became a part of the English and Spanish praise and worship teams on the Smith Unit.

I eventually made parole after first being refused and set-off for a year. I wasn't sure where God wanted me to parole to. I could have gone back home as I had been offered help from a cousin of mine. She was willing to give me a car and allow me to stay at her house until I was able to get my own place, but something in my heart told me that going back home was not what God wanted me to do. The last time I went home on parole didn't work out well.

So, I thought I was headed to Dallas, Texas, when my Chaplain called me into his office saying that he had referred me to a one year, Christian discipleship program called Life Abundant Transformation Program (LATP). LATP is a program that helps men coming out of prison make a stress-free transition into the free world by supplying both spiritual and financial support to those who are recommended, screened and accepted into the program. This "pay it forward" program was the very thing for which I had been praying. I knew from the beginning this was where God wanted me to go, so I went there when I was released in 2019.

The program is housed at Kingdom Towers in Lubbock, TX, where I ended up staying for almost 19 months and where I was blessed in so many ways. In April, 2021, I moved from Lubbock to Amarillo, TX, where I am living a great, God-given life with my family. Through the grace of God, I have been able to share some of my experiences and perspective with many others. My hope is that those who may be burdened with the same type of concerns and worries that once held me in bondage would find freedom and encouragement through my experience and my testimony. I have dealt with all of the issues, restrictions, and stigmas that come with any sex-offender charge and have found that God can make a way where it seems there is no way.

At the time of this writing, I am happily married with a beautiful wife and family the Lord has given me. Now I have a completely new life where I am enjoying serving God. No matter what you may have gone through or may be going through now, or what others may say about you or your future, please understand and know that God is the Author of your life and the Definer of who you are. Nothing in your past, present or future can stop the life God has in store for you except you. There is hope! There is life! There is a good, God-given future in store for you in Christ Jesus!

I love you all and pray that my experiences will be a blessing and reminder of God's ability to transform and give new life to all those who place their trust and lives into His hands. May the Lord give you the desires of your heart, as your heart's desire is to always bring Him Glory.

GOD NEVER GIVES UP

By Duane Brecheisen

My name is Duane. I am happy to be able to share this testimony with you. I hope that it will benefit you in your walk with or to Christ Jesus. I am nervous sharing my testimony, but I have come to know that silence on some things is how the evil one gains access to us and that the sharing of our experience, strength, and hope is the best way for us all to lift each other up. We are as sick as our secrets.

For most of my life I was a solitary type of person. I had four brothers and one sister, but we were raised to be independent and not to impose upon others. This made me very self-centered and I was not really concerned about anyone but me. Even when I got married and had my first son, my life was centered around me and what I wanted.

My first wife, pregnant with our first son, simply came up missing one day. To my shame, I wasn't really too concerned about this. I had married her only because she had become pregnant and I did not (and do not) believe that abortion is an appropriate answer to unwanted pregnancy. When the adoption papers came in the mail from an attorney, I signed them and sent them back; forever giving up my firstborn son to another. I pray today that he has found a loving family and enjoys a life that fulfills him and is full of the joy and blessings that God has for him.

When I entered my second marriage, I was less self-centered, but I really had no clear idea of what to do in a relationship or how to be a father, so I spent all my time working and trying to "be a man" and provide for my family. I had a better idea what this meant, as I was raised by a loving father who spent his entire life doing just that. I thought this was working out alright, but still I did not give the attention to my family it needed to be a family. My second son was born and I felt that I had finally stumbled upon a solution to the emptiness and un-fulfillment I had been familiar with for most of my life.

All this time I did not have a personal relationship with God or Jesus Christ. Sure, I had been to church and even been baptized; but trusting in the Lord to provide for me and my family, listening to the prompting of the Spirit of God, acting on the leading of the Spirit.... This was not part of the plan. I was in control and I intended to stay there. I had been raised to be self-sufficient and to always be in control of my life, and I thought I was doing a good job of it.

I was also carrying around baggage from my past. I had a bucket-load of issues in my relationships which the evil one was able to twist and distort into a host of promiscuous, predatory behaviors sexually. This lifestyle led me to committing sexual acts and eventually being convicted of sexually assaulting my second wife and being sent to prison for three years.

Upon my release from prison the first time, I became more predatory, acting my pain and confusion out in sexual acts that again resulted in me being incarcerated for sexual assaults; this time in Texas... with a life sentence. I had given my life over to a choice for evil, acting out the will of the one who would destroy not only myself, but as many people as he could get me to take with me into the abyss of despair and ruin. I was on the road and on the run from everything I had ever been taught was good and heading straight to my own hell right here on earth. I got exactly what I was looking for, and exactly what I deserved, when it all finally caught up with me in Texas.

I entered the Texas Department of Corrections in November of 1987, rebellious and angry. I embraced the fact that I was home now, that I would most likely never leave prison.

For many years I involved myself in activities that benefitted myself, still living as I had for all of my life. I still did not care that I might hurt others or myself. I knew about God and the devil–who doesn't these days in America? But, I had always believed in myself, relied on myself, and never considered that anyone could and would care to make a way for me to be happy or meet my needs. I looked to the world, science, material possessions, and intellectual knowledge (facts) to provide for my needs. I became very good at denying that the spiritual realm existed and believed that I was evil and could never change. I was not the badass that controlled situations with brute force, or the genius who controlled situations with psychology, but I was a survivor and could usually find some way to fulfill my wants and needs.

I manipulated the prison society to my advantage, carving out a niche for myself providing services to those who could afford to pay me what I wanted for those services. I spent some time in medium custody, but

I avoided Ad-Seg (solitary confinement) because I was good at talking my way out of trouble and telling the prison authorities what they wanted to hear. This helped me to "get by" in a system that did nothing for the men subjected to the use and abuse that is often prevalent in penal institutions, but it was a life full of strife and constant struggle to come out on top. Most of the time I felt that I was doing okay, but I was only participating in a give and take lifestyle, hoping that it was less give than take.

I have come to believe that God reached out to me in prison, although I had not yet sought Him or paid any heed to the appeals of the people who reached out to me trying to teach me about salvation and Christ. Many times, in retrospect, what I merely attributed to luck or happenstance, was Jesus Christ intervening for me, saving me from the worst of the evil one's plans and my own tendencies to sabotage my life. After a few years, I began to seek change. I was tired of the way my life was going, the constant rollercoaster that is prison life, and began to seek another way.

A friend of mine invited me to an AA meeting. I agreed to attend and went. I was hoping that I could gain some relief from the hassle that my life had become. Fortunately, God had placed a counselor at my unit who was sincere and able to reach me in my confusion and delusions. I attended AA for a few years, claiming the doorknob as my higher power, when one day something just clicked, Jesus Christ had become real to me in a way that I had never experienced before. I can't explain this change, but I began to see myself and those around me in a different way, not as something to be used to meet my own wants and needs, but as fellow travelers on a journey. I did not at this time become dedicated to Christ or anything, but I began to question my role as I had seen it in society and life.

I began to explore religion, hoping to find a religion that would allow me to continue to do pretty much what I wanted and still give me a feeling that I was no longer alone. I attended as many of the religious activities that would let me in, and never really committed my life to any of them. I was still not ready to step out in faith and let God and His Holy Spirit lead my life. I experienced the Love of God over and over again, at Church meeting, in personal conversations with believers in population… over and over God reached out to me, while all this time I held back, hesitant to accept the healing and salvation He offered. In 1996, I attended a Kairos walk (an inside spiritual retreat weekend) and began to feel the spirit of God moving in my life.

I also began to explore the self-help programs that were offered. There again the Lord placed a person in my life who would demonstrate God's Love for me time and time again, teaching me to get out of myself and see others as not something I could use to get what I wanted, but as human beings themselves who had many of the same hopes, fears, and hang-ups I did. I learned from this messenger of God to care for my body, mind, and spirit as well as the well-being of those around me.

I came to believe that I was a spiritual being, traveling with other spiritual beings. I still did not fully accept God as my God, although at AA I did acknowledge Him as my Higher Power. This transformation would not occur in me until God reached out and demonstrated to me that he is able to do for me the things that I thought could never be done–He granted me parole after thirty-three years in prison. I never expected that. I had even written a letter to the parole board explaining to them that I was okay with the fact that I was never going to get out of prison. I began to listen to His Spirit, to seek His will for me and to question my belief that I could be in control of my life and not make a complete mess of it.

I also came to believe that the truth I had always known was in fact The Truth. That evil existed not as me, but in me only if I allowed it. Free will is the ability to choose to rebel against the will of God. I am free to allow myself to work the will of the one who would place himself on a level with God, exalting himself above all things. I came to the realization that if I could live my life for this evil being and work his will in my life, than I could live my life for God, working His will and seeking Him.

Think about it, if you have tails on your coin, then you also have heads. If there is a being who will advocate evil through me, then there is also a Being who will advocate good through me. I could continue to make the same choices, but I knew now that I would not get any result but what I had been getting all my life. This was presented to me in AA as the definition of insanity, to continue to do the same thing expecting a different result. I could continue to believe that I was in control, that I knew what was best for me, sure, but this was the lie that the evil one used for all my life to get me to do his will, and he comes only to steal, destroy and kill.

God would reach out one more time to me before my release. Before I could be released I had to complete a nine month Sexual Offender Treatment Program. Before I began this I was evaluated for civil commitment. I felt that I was sure to be committed. I had multiple sexual offenses: one against a family member, and two against victims I did not know. By any definition, I was a sexual predator. The only thing left to decide was would I be returned to prison, placed in an institution for the criminally insane, or released.

I never really felt that release was an option, but God had other plans. On May 20, 2020, I walked out of the Walls Unit of the Texas Department of Criminal Justice without shackles for the first time in thirty-three years. Miracles had occurred in my life that I never thought would happen.

The Lord had one more surprise for me before I walked out of the Walls unit. Up until the time I received my gate money I thought I was going to the halfway house in El Paso, Texas. I had heard all the talk about El Paso, and, depending on your choices it was either a great place to go to or a trap waiting to spring you right back to the Walls and prison. God had again placed a person in my life who would work His will for me to accomplish change in me.

I had been in contact with a Christian transitional program facility in Lubbock, Texas, for a few months, hoping to avoid going to a state halfway house. I had an acceptance letter but could not seem to get it to the Parole board, something always came up unexplainably wrong. The Parole ladies on the Terell and the Walls Units were very helpful but could not seem to get it done. Somehow Mr. Steve Taylor, the manager of Kingdom Towers in Lubbock, Texas, reached out to the parole office in Lubbock and worked with them to get the Parole board in Austin to allow me to parole to Kingdom Towers. This final attack of the evil one to keep me in his grasp had not worked thanks to the dedicated work of a man doing God's work for me.

It had finally been enough to reach me. Before I got on the bus in Huntsville I dedicated my life to Christ Jesus. Mine was not a public or ceremonial expression of my decision, but a private decision. The way I saw things, who else but Christ could have done the things that in a few short years had transformed my life's situation so completely? No other being I had been exposed to during my search for meaning and answers had so much as hinted that such things were possible.

Certainly not me. The odds of this all happening by chance were, to me, as high as the odds for the spontaneous creation of all the myriad life needed for the Earth to evolve as it had to reach the point that I would need and receive this blessing. One such coincidence I could believe, but twice was just too much random chance for me to accept.

My choice was celebrated on a Greyhound bus from Huntsville to Dallas, where I got a taste of what awaited me in Lubbock. What an awesome and inspiring ride it was. Not only was I celebrating my freedom from incarceration, but I was seeing myself and the whole world through different eyes. I finally had someone I felt I could turn to, to talk to, who would not only listen, but would actively work on my behalf. And I knew that even if He did not work in a way I had hoped He would, He would always work in a way that was to my benefit, according to His will for me and my life.

God has continued to reach out to me and to bless me as I have reentered into society. I have been so blessed by God that I cannot believe it. Yes, it has been difficult at times, but as I have continued to be faithful to Him, He has been faithful to me. I have stumbled often, but He always reaches down to lift me up. So long as I continue to get up and follow Him, I will continue to be blessed.

CLOSER THAN A BROTHER

By Russell Stewart, as told to Don Castleberry

My name is Rusty Stewart and I am an ex-convict and a former sex offender. I spent thirty-two and one half years in Texas prisons. The following is my testimony of God's goodness and grace to me.

I grew up in a good home. There was a man I met through church who God would use later in my life, Don Enger. I first met him in Shallowater, Texas where I lived and went to high school. Don knew my sister and me. I was in Don's class which he taught to my youth group at the Methodist church. As I grew up, I lost track of Don and never tried to contact him.

I pretty much turned my back on God to live life my way. During high school and afterwards, I was wild and out of control. At the time I was arrested, I was married and had a son two years old. I picked up my first case of aggravated sexual assault in my early twenties, did a short jail term and my sentence was probated.

That short jail sentence didn't slow me down as I still did pretty much whatever I wanted. Little did I know then what my evil actions would cost me. So, it wasn't long thereafter that I committed aggravated sexual assault again. I was young, dumb, and I was serving satan. I had no regard for women. I had no regard for God.

I started my journey to prison on January 1, 1988, when I turned myself in to Lubbock County law enforcement. That was my last taste of freedom until my release from the Texas Department of Criminal Justice (TDCJ) on August 6, 2019. A police officer was transporting me to county jail, and told me to look up to the sky, because it would be the last time I would see the sky as a free man.

I went to trial later that year after spending nine months in Lubbock County jail, was found guilty, and was sentenced to life in prison. At my sentencing, my wife told me that she would wait for me. I looked at her and said, "Why would you do that? You might as well get a divorce and go on with your life."

TDCJ picked me up to "catch chain" to Huntsville, TX, on my 24th birthday, September 27, 1988. Because my charge branded me as a sex offender I was scared to death of going to a maximum security Texas prison.

When I arrived at the back sally port to the prison, I was immediately taken to diagnostics for intake. I was stripped searched, and issued jumpers until I was assigned to a unit which was Beto 1 of TDCJ. For the next 24 years, I learned the ropes, how to get along with people. Don't make anybody mad, stay to yourself, and mind your own business.

During that 24-year period, I had a ten year time out in administrative segregation. I was 23 hours a day by myself in a cell with one hour a day exercise. During that twenty-four years I never attended prison church except for the Christmas program. However, after I transferred to the Smith Unit in Lamesa, TX, I began to attend church but not right away. Time went by. I attained my associates' degree in 2012 after seven years of study. My degree is associates of art.

In 2009, after I had been in prison for many years, Don Enger (my former youth director in the Methodist Church who I mentioned earlier) happened to see my sister and asked about me. She told him I had been in prison a long time. Little did I know that after thirty years Don would contact me in prison and came to visit me at the Smith Unit in Lamesa, TX.

Those visits were such a blessing to me. Sometimes he would bring another friend. They showed me the unconditional love of God. Don gave me a *Life in the Spirit Study Bible*, which I began to read, but I did not really believe that I would ever get out, so I thought then, "What's the use?" But God...

At the Smith Unit I applied to attend the Kairos Walk and was accepted. It is a three-day spiritual retreat weekend held inside the facility with forty prisoners. During that three days, the Holy Spirit began to draw me to the love and grace of Jesus Christ, and I was blown away. After 26 years of living in prison, with all the evil happening, I accepted Jesus as my Lord and Savior. The love of godly men overwhelmed me, my heart melted, and I was born again.

My friend Don Enger visited me often. He loved me. He encouraged me. He was like a second father to me. I loved him. I believed what he told me. He discipled me in the Word of God and never gave up on me. Don began to talk to many people in authority with TDCJ about me and my sentences.

In 2015, my third time for parole came up. I had stacked sentences, which means that I had to parole one before I could begin to serve the other sentence. My sentences were life plus a 99-year sentence. At that time, I never believed that I would ever be free.

Time went on. In 2016 I was shipped to Robertson Unit in Abilene, Texas. I did two years there. During this time Don Enger was continuing to work diligently for my parole. He had already talked to many parole officers, people in high authority including the chairman of TDCJ parole concerning my case. I was transferred to Hightower Unit in Dayton, Texas in 2018. I still did not believe that I would ever see freedom.

My cellmate was a Christian and we began to study the Bible together. For nine months we were in the same cell. We studied the Bible together, we prayed together, and we prayed for each other. My favorite scripture came to be Jeremiah 29:11, where God says, "For I know the plans I have for you, plans to prosper you and not to harm you, plans to give you a hope and a future..."

In March 2018, I was called to the unit parole office. I was told that my case had been considered for parole. I was told that upon the condition of completing a sex offender program, I would be paroled. What a miracle, God granted me parole! God had used my childhood youth director, Don Enger, to help secure my release.

I completed that program successfully, and on August 6, 2019, I walked out of the Walls Unit in Huntsville, Texas as a parolee. I looked up at the sky and thanked God for the miracle that He had given me.

The next day I arrived at a Christian transitional program facility called Kingdom Towers in Lubbock, Texas. Once again, my friend Don Enger stepped up and helped me get established as a free man.

My case required me to wear an ankle monitor for one year, which restricted my movement. I could not go anywhere unless I was cleared by my parole officer, and even then it had to be on a definite schedule.

Behold, another miracle from God happened! My parole officer recommended that my monitor be removed, and it was after only 60 days. Praise God! Surely the favor of God was on me. I thanked my God for His care of me once again.

My first job was as a helper with a remodeling contractor for two months. My second job was with a trim carpenter, which only lasted one month.

Through another miracle, I began to clean properties for a contractor. Through that experience, I was injured with sciatic nerve issues and could not walk. Through another miracle, God healed me totally.

I then began my own business as a house cleaner, which I have today – Rusty's Immaculate Cleaning Service. As of Spring, 2021, I have now been self- employed for fourteen months. God is so good!

I began attending church upon arrival at Kingdom Towers in August, 2019. The following February, Don Enger baptized me at Trinity Church in Lubbock. I still attend that church.

Don Enger started encouraging me to give my testimony at various places, and he set up appointments for me. So far, I have given my testimony at many places, including the Gideons, various churches, prime-timers at Trinity Church Lubbock, with other opportunities coming up soon. I have been warmly received by everyone, and thank God for His care for me in honoring Him through my testimony. I also thank God that I facilitate two classes at Kingdom Towers, including a Bible class, and a Celebrate Recovery class.

God has also miraculously restored relationships in my life. As soon as I was released I was able to visit my mother who has dementia. My sister Cindy said, "Mom, look who is here!" She did not recognize me at first, then another God miracle happened. It seemed as if God renewed her mind and we were able to have a two-hour lucid conversation.

When I arrived at Kingdom Towers, I had not seen my son since 2009, when he came to visit me when I was on Smith Unit. We had a two-hour visit there. It was a contact visit, so we hugged and had a good talk.

My son, Chase, who is now 34, came to see me at Kingdom Towers about three months after I arrived. We had a good visit. I am praying now that our relationship will deepen between us to the point that one day we will serve God together.

As of the time of this writing, I have been free for almost two years. I have been so blessed in so many ways. God has been so good to me!

The Bible says, "...there is a friend who sticks closer than a brother." (Proverbs 18:24) In my story, certainly Don Enger has been closer than a brother. Thank you, Don, in fact you are like a father to me!

I am "all in" for God. One of my strongest desires is to return to prison as a ministry volunteer. I want to speak to a prisoner in the crowd who has doubts that God would ever do anything for him. I was once that man. I believed that I would never get out of prison.

BUT HERE I AM. I am living proof that miracles didn't only happen in Biblical times, they happen today.

TRANSFORMATION
EXAMPLE

The "Old Man"

Six Months before Prison (2007)

Stephen Canup

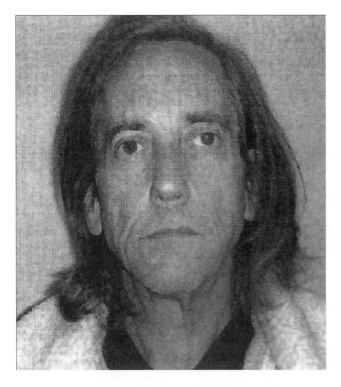

Guilty and condemned by sin to death

Romans 6:23 "For the wages of sin is death...

Guilty of these sins against God, others and self:

Addictions to drugs, alcohol, sex, pornography, praise of men, work

Pride	Perversion	Depravity	Confusion
Worry	Idolatry	Reprobation	Lying
Fear	Selfishness	Un-forgiveness	Conceit
Depression	Judgment	Immorality	Intellectualism
Hopelessness	Self-hate	Self-abuse	Humanism
Anxiety	Resentment	Bitterness	Shame
Profanity	Regret	Thievery	Remorse
Fornication	Anger	Adultery	Guilt
Lustful desires	Covetousness	Sexual identity	Offense

The sinful and cursed life I was living before prison resulted in me being:

- Homeless, living on the streets of Nashville, TN, for 3 years prior to prison.
- Unemployed for 7 years prior to incarceration.
- Broke after having filed for bankruptcy twice.
- Destitute with all my earthly possessions contained in 1 hanging garment bag in the prison's property room awaiting the day of my release.
- Desolate having abandoned all family and friends, leaving me lonely and utterly forsaken.
- Depressed so deeply by these life conditions that I had attempted suicide several times.
- Hopeless and absolutely convinced nothing would ever change or get better in any way.

The "New Man"

One Year after Prison (2012)

Stephen Canup

A Free Man – Alive in Christ

...but the gift of God is eternal life in Christ Jesus our Lord."

Romans 6:23

"I have been crucified with Christ and I no longer live, but Christ lives in me. The life I now live in the body, I live by

faith in the Son of God, who loved me and gave himself for me." (Gal. 2:20)

"Therefore if any is (ingrafted) in Christ, the Messiah, he is (a new creature altogether), a new creation; the old (previous moral and spiritual condition) has passed away. Behold, the fresh and new has come!" (II Cor. 5:17, AMP)

"So if the Son sets you free, you will be free indeed" (John 8:36)

The new life in Christ that began in prison in 2009 has brought many blessings. As of early 2017, some of these abundant life realities include:

- My spiritual re-birth April 20, 2009!!!
- Restored relationships with every family member.
- A mentor and accountability partner, Don Castleberry, who speaks the truth in love.
- Acceptance instead of rejection.
- Joy and hope instead of depression and hopelessness.
- Purpose and passion to help set others free.
- Peace, boldness and confidence instead of anxiety and fear.
- The righteousness of Christ Jesus instead of perversion and depravity.
- Love and compassion for others instead of selfishness and self-hate.
- Freedom from addictions to alcohol, drugs, pornography, smoking and gambling.
- A tongue of blessings and respect instead of pride, criticism and profanity.

- A beautiful, three bedroom, two bath home provided rent-free except for utilities.
- Three late-model vehicles have been provided to me free, in great condition, with low mileage.
- A house full of good furniture, and a closet full of good clothes.
- Debt-free, with also some money in savings.
- A renewed mind free of all the bad effects of addictions and depression.
- Good health.
- Mature Christians I can call for prayer or advice anytime about anything.
- Licensed and ordained in 2012 as a minister of the Gospel of Jesus Christ.
- President of Freedom in Jesus Prison Ministries.

JAIL-HOUSE RELIGION
"THE REAL THING" OR "A CHEAP IMITATION"?

Stephen E. Canup, 2010, while incarcerated

"Jail-House Religion".... How many times have we heard that phrase? It's usually in a mocking way. Is it "the real thing" or "a cheap imitation"?

Can someone really find God in a jail or prison? Is God close enough to us here to hear our sincere cry? Can we really be heard by Him as we commit, or re-dedicate, our hearts to walk with Christ? What does God say about people like us in His Word? Can He actually use a convict, who turns his life around, to advance the cause of His Kingdom?

We know what "society" says and thinks about us – they call us misfits, outcasts and career criminals. For the most part, they despise us. They think that we are worthless, dangerous and not capable of changing our ways. They are ashamed of us, afraid of us and would like to forget us. When they lock us up we are "out of sight, out of mind". We are at the very bottom of the social ladder – like the bottom of a dark empty well with no ladder to climb out. How low can we go and still find God?

When we are as low as we can go, and think that the only "light at the end of the tunnel" is a train headed our way, what do we do?

When we finally wake up one day and realize we are sick and tired of being locked up again and again because of our own stupid actions, wrong decisions, and addictions, who do we turn to?

Isn't this the time and place that makes the most sense to cry out to God?

Think about the story of "The Prodigal Son" – he was eating, sleeping and working among the pigs in the muck and mud. The Bible says in Luke 15:17, that he finally "came to his senses", saw the error of his ways, desired forgiveness, and turned back to go home to his father. Sometimes, God uses the worst of conditions at the bottom of our own miry pit to get our attention. Psalm 118:5 says, "In my anguish I cried to the Lord, and He answered me by setting me free."

In Luke 19:10, Jesus said He "...came to seek and to save what was lost." The religious leaders of the day wanted to know why He ate with and ministered to "sinners". Where are plenty of us lost sinners? Locked up in prison. Jesus is seeking to save us!

In here we are sober and in our right minds. We are "still". If we listen, we can hear Him here!

SEEK THE LORD

God tells us if we seek Him (look hard for Him), we will find Him! It does not matter where we are, how old we are, what our problems are – if we seek Him, He will be found by us.

Is. 55:6-7–"Seek the Lord while He may be found: Call on Him while He is near. Let the wicked forsake his way and the evil man his thoughts. Let him turn to the Lord, and he will have mercy on him, and to our God, for He will freely pardon."

Jer. 29:11-14-"For I know the plans I have for you, declares the Lord, plans to prosper you and not to harm you, plans to give you hope and a future. Then you will call upon me and come and pray to me and I will listen to you. You will seek me and find me when you seek me with all your heart. I will be found by you, declares the Lord, and will bring you back from captivity..."

In other words, when we seek God with all of our heart we will find Him – even when we are locked up.

WE ARE IN GOOD COMPANY

Throughout the entire Bible, time after time, we find God using some of the most unlikely people to accomplish His will to advance His Kingdom. He has used murderers, adulterers, thieves, lowly shepherds, hated tax collectors; and, a lot of them had, at one time or another, been in some form of confinement or captivity.

But these men repented, committed their lives to God, and cried out to Him from their own miserable circumstances. People like Peter, Paul, Samson, James, John the Baptist, Joseph, and Jeremiah had been incarcerated just like us. Leaders like Moses, David, and Jacob – who were once murderers, adulterers and thieves–were used mightily once they called on God and turned their lives back to Him. Even Jesus was arrested and put on trial.

God does not care about your record. Unlike men, God does not discriminate against the down-trodden, the lowly, the forgotten – we who are labeled as felons, sex offenders, prisoners, convicts or inmates.

GOD HAS A SPECIAL LOVE FOR PEOPLE LIKE US

God must have a special love and attention reserved for people like us – prisoners, convicts, inmates, and captives. In fact, Strong's Concordance listed over 340 verses where the word "prison", "prisoner", "captive" or captivity" is a key word.

FOR EXAMPLE:

> Ps. 102:19-20 – "The Lord looked down...from Heaven...to hear the groans of the prisoners..."

> Ps. 69:33 – "The Lord... does not despise His captive people..."

> Ps. 146:7 – "The Lord sets prisoners free."

> Zech. 9:11-12 – "I will free your prisoners from the waterless pit...O prisoners of hope; even now I announce that I will restore twice as much to you."

> Matt. 25:36 – Jesus said, "...I was in prison and you came and visited me."

And in one of His first talks in the synagogue, after Satan tempted Him in the wilderness, Jesus quoted:

> Is. 61:1 "...the Lord has anointed me to preach good news to the poor. He has sent me to bind up the broken-hearted, to proclaim freedom for the captives and release from darkness for the prisoners..."

Jeremiah, one of the most important and Holy prophets in the Old Testament, was himself falsely accused and was held as a prisoner at the bottom of an old cistern – a hole like a well–dark, damp and deep in the ground.

Jer. 38:6 – "So they took Jeremiah and put him into the cistern... they lowered Jeremiah by ropes into the cistern; it had no water in it, only mud, and Jeremiah sank down into the mud."

But God did not leave him there! Later on, in Jer. 38:11-13, God used a Babylonian ruler, an enemy, to appeal to the King on Jeremiah's behalf. He got permission to pull Jeremiah up out of the pit, not long before he would have starved to death.

GOD HAS PLENTY OF EXPERIENCE PULLING PEOPLE UP

Just like he did for Jeremiah, God has plenty of experience pulling people up out of their own miry, dark, damp, deep pit. David, a man after God's own heart, must have known exactly what it was like. See if you can see yourself in David's own "pit experience":

Ps. 69:1-3, 5, 14-17 – "Save me, O God, for the waters have come up to my neck. I sink in the miry depths, where there is no foothold. I have come into the deep waters; the floods engulf me. I am worn out calling for help; my throat is parched. My eyes fail, looking for my God... You know my folly, O God; my guilt is not hidden from you... Rescue me from the mire, do not let me sink; deliver me from those who hate me, from the deep waters. Do not let the floodwaters engulf me or the depths swallow me up or the pit close its mouth over me. Answer me, O Lord, out of the goodness of your love; in your great mercy turn to me. Do not hide your face from your servant; answer me quickly, for I am in trouble".

Ps. 40:1-4a – "I waited patiently for the Lord; He turned to me and heard my cry. He lifted me out of the slimy pit, out of the mud and mire; He set my feet on a rock and gave me a firm place to stand. He put a new song in my mouth, a hymn of praise to our God. Many will see and fear and put their trust in the Lord. Blessed is the man who makes the Lord His trust..."

Not only will God rescue you, and pull you up out of your own pit, but He can use your example, your story, and your testimony to bring others to Him!

"YOU WEREN'T READING YOUR BIBLE ON THE STREET"

Most people don't know what these scriptures say about how important prisoners are to God and His work, and how much He loves them. So, many inmates taunt Christians with stuff like, "You weren't reading your Bible on the street"; or, "You weren't going to church or chapel services before they locked you up"; or, "Man, that's just that old jail-house religion, it will wear off pretty soon. It's not real. It's just the same old fake stuff we've seen before."

In some ways they're right. I don't know about you, but if I had been caught up in God's Word instead of my addictions, I probably wouldn't have ended up here. If I had been going to church every week instead of going out to beg, borrow or steal enough to get my next hit, I probably wouldn't have ended up here. I'm sick and tired of places like this. I want to be a better man for my family. I need Jesus. I need to change. I want to change.

DO YOU HAVE "THE REAL THING"?

"Jail-House Religion" can either be "the real thing" or "a cheap imitation". All of us have seen imitation, "knock-off" products – fake Nike tennis shoes, imitation Air-Jordan's, fake designer handbags like Gucci, etc. You can tell the fakes over time, maybe not so much at first, but over time the imitation breaks down, falls apart and gets thrown away. We don't use it anymore. It becomes clear why it was so cheap to begin with.

Unlike when we might have been tricked into buying a fake "knock-off", in our new relationship with God, we determine, through our own actions, habits and beliefs, whether we get "the real thing" or "a cheap imitation".

How will we, and others, be able to tell whether our own personal experiences with "Jail-House Religion" result in "the real thing" or just "a cheap imitation"?

Let's compare some of the characteristics of each one:

"THE REAL THING"	VS.	"A CHEAP IMITATION"
• We try to be serious about it and consistently try to do the right thing.		• We are "on again, off again", inconsistent, like we are "playing with God".
• We allocate regular, significant time daily to God's Word.		• We are too tired or too busy to try to read even the one page devotional from "Our Daily Bread".
• People notice good, positive changes in the way we talk and act.		• By the way we talk or act, our friends might never know or even guess that we are following Christ.
• We have real joy, peace and more genuine love.		• We still hold on to anger, depression and hate.

"THE REAL THING"	VS.	"A CHEAP IMITATION"

- When we are released, our Bibles and God go with us.

- When we are released we leave our Bibles behind on our bunks or one of the tables. We leave God behind too.

- After release, we find a good pastor, join the church and attend faithfully.

- After release, we keep "intending" to go to church but we never get around to it.

- We will have fellowship daily with other Christians, and find a Bible study group to challenge us.

- We go right back to our old friends and hang out in the same places.

CHOOSE THE REAL THING

Personally, I want "the real thing". God got my attention. I want the rest of my life to be the opposite of my recent past. I don't want to keep coming back here.

They say insanity is doing the same old thing over and over and over again and expecting different results. I might be crazy, but I am not yet insane! When I finally "came to my senses" after my first ten months of incarceration, like "The Prodigal Son", I wanted to go back to my Heavenly Father. I decided I was going to do something different, so I could be different, so I could finally make a difference in my own life, the lives of my family, and in my community.

When it comes to "Jail-House Religion", I want "The Real Thing" – a personal relationship with Jesus Christ as my Savior and Lord! Each of us gets to make our own decision. Have you made this decision? Have you decided to go "all in and all out" for Jesus?

Be encouraged, be strong, be blessed – choose "The Real Thing"! There is no better time to cry out for God. He will hear you. His Word says you are special to Him. He will help you. He loves you wherever, and however, and whoever you are now. You do not have to "change" before you find Jesus. He will change you if you let Him. Just go to Him. He will take care of the rest.

STEPHEN CANUP'S JOURNEY

"From Park Avenue... to Park Bench... to Prison"

A PERSONAL TESTIMONY OF GOD'S GRACE AND MERCY

Stephen E. Canup

I never dreamed my life testimony would include a period of nearly three years in prison starting at age 56. Yet, I really should not be surprised since I had been running from God, and living against Him, for 20 years. In fact, I had not truly served Him for 40 years. When asked, I told others I was "a Christian", but who did I think I was kidding? I only deceived myself, not God, and I reaped what I sowed (Gal. 6:7-8).

I can only blame myself. I alone accept full responsibility for my actions. I definitely do not blame God. He didn't cause this. He didn't leave me or forsake me – I was the one who left Him. Neither can I blame my "environment" or my family. I was raised in a middle-class home in a good neighborhood by both parents who were dedicated Christians. I cannot blame the justice system. As a first-time offender, I would never have even been locked up for nearly three years if I had only initially obeyed the terms of my probation.

It was my own fault. I gave myself over to worldly temptations, pursuits and pleasures. My addictions to drugs, alcohol, sex and pornography only made matters much worse. Where did I first "go wrong"?

ON TOP OF THE WORLD

Twenty years earlier, I was living "the American Dream". I had what, in the world's eyes, was a marvelously successful life. In 1987, at age 35, I was at the top of my profession as a CPA earning a salary well into the six-figures. I had an office on the 27th floor of a high-rise office building on Park Avenue in New York City. I was a partner with the world's largest accounting firm. I had been blessed with a wonderful, Godly wife and a healthy infant son. I would soon have a new, custom built home. The vehicles we drove had no loans against them. My credit record was spotless. I had credit cards with over $100,000 available credit and, except for the mortgage I would have on our new home, I was totally free of consumer debt. By any worldly standard, I was "on top of the world".

Outwardly, I was the definition of success. Inwardly, however, I was lost, confused, bored, empty and restless (Eccl 2:10-11). I was addicted to pride, success, and money. I lived my life to garner the acceptance and good opinions of others. I realize now I had everything but the one thing that mattered–I did not have Jesus. I was not thankful. I did not desire or seek God. I thought I was wise, but I was a fool (Rom. 1:21-22). My conceit, impatience, greed, selfishness and pride were about to destroy my life (Prov. 16:18).

THE LONG DOWNWARD SPIRAL

In 1989, I suddenly, foolishly and selfishly left my wife and son to pursue worldly desires, fame and riches in Nashville's music business. I became my own "god", determined to create and control my own life. For this vanity and foolish pride, God gave me over to my own desires, lusts and addictions. It was a gradual, but steady, descent over 20 years into sinfulness, depravity and reprobation (Rom 1:24-32).

It didn't take too long to see that I had made a fatal error. Trying to "break in" to the music publishing and writing business was near impossible. The odds of success for me were about the same as me competing in Hollywood for a part in a movie against established actors like Brad Pitt, Leonardo DiCaprio or, back then, Tom Cruise. How stupid I was. For the first time in my life I had failed – and failed miserably. All the money I had, and all I could borrow, had been invested foolishly. I lost it all.

I experienced addictions to alcohol, marijuana, crack cocaine, gambling, sex and pornography. For many years, I was severely and almost continuously in deep depression and often contemplated suicide. There were several failed suicide attempts. Unashamedly, I participated in almost every form of sexual immorality and perversion. I was a spiritual, mental, emotional and financial wreck. I filed bankruptcy twice. I was diagnosed as having bi-polar disorder.

I was so empty inside for so many years. In spite of everything I tried, nothing filled the void in my soul. I felt unworthy of love and, over time, I had pushed away every friend and family member. I was without hope and without God in my world (Eph. 2:12).

From 2002-2008, I was unemployed and existed only by the kindness of strangers and one friend, who loved me in spite of myself. He allowed me to stay rent-free with him for three years. Eventually I alienated even him. I got an apartment and a menial job for a few months (after I could no longer stay with him), but was soon fired and homeless. It was 2006.

I lived in a tent on an undeveloped wooded hillside in South Nashville for 1½years. Then I lived for 6 months at the Nashville Rescue Mission – a homeless shelter for men. I was there when I was arrested in May, 2008, for violating the terms of my probation. My six-year probated sentence was revoked and I was sent to CCA-Nashville's medium-security prison to serve my time.

Life looked totally hopeless, and I was convinced nothing would ever get better. To me, my life was over, but a merciful and loving God rescued me in spite of myself. Thank God, He was not finished with me yet. I see now that He had His own plan for my life, but He would not begin to reveal it until I finally realized and admitted what a mess and failure I had made after I made myself "god" of my life. I needed to humble myself and submit to Him. I had to surrender.

JAIL-HOUSE RELIGION

As you can safely conclude by now, I definitely was not following Jesus before I went to prison. I didn't find Him in prison. He wasn't lost. I was. He found me.

My first act of submission was to ask for a Bible from the Chaplain – a Gideon New Testament which I read daily for about 15 minutes. I remember how hesitant I was at first to openly read my Bible and go to Chapel services. I had already heard plenty of remarks about other Christians in prison regarding "Jail-House Religion". So, for the first ten months I only read my Bible privately for a few minutes each night. I did not attend Chapel services. I watched TV, played cards and read a lot of spy novels and westerns. None of this got me out of my deep depression or made any positive change in me. Time passed slowly.

I eventually realized I had finally reached bottom. I could not go any lower. I had lost everything. I felt absolutely hopeless. On top of everything else, my crime was "solicitation of a minor" – a charge I picked up during a stretch of five days without sleep fueled by my addictions to crack cocaine, pornography and alcohol. I did some incredibly stupid things resulting in me now being branded as a "sex offender". I now realize God does not see one sin worse than another, but my hopelessness caused me to see it only in the way it is viewed by society.

After 10 months in prison, I finally "came to my senses" like the Prodigal Son (Luke 15:11-24). When I finally surrendered to God, and cried out in true humility and brokenness, He heard me. He lifted me out of the miry pit of hopelessness and despair. He placed my feet solidly on His Rock–Jesus (Psalm 40:1-3).

On April 20, 2009, my 57th birthday, I re-dedicated my life to Jesus Christ. I was re-baptized while I was in prison too. I confessed my sins, sincerely repented, and asked Jesus to take over my life. What a heavy burden of guilt, shame, remorse and embarrassment I had been carrying. As I finally submitted to Him, these burdens were lifted off my soul and spirit.

Even though I was still locked up, I was "free on the inside"! Jesus became not only my Savior, but I made Him truly my Lord and put Him in charge. I decided I was going to go "all in and all out" for Jesus–a decision I have never once regretted, not even for a minute!

As I began to read the Bible, I became convinced that through Jesus, my future could be totally new and different from my past. When I realized that God could find me and change me even in prison, I wanted to know as much as I could about pursuing a relationship with Him. I ignored snide and sarcastic comments about "Jail-House Religion";

"You weren't going to church before you got here, why are going to Chapel services here, choirboy?"; and, "You weren't reading your Bible on the street, why are you reading it in here?"

I knew God was real because He was changing me gradually, but completely, from the inside out. The changes I felt were not "forced" by me, but were occurring primarily as a result of spending more time deliberately in His Word and prayerfully in His presence.

My boldness and commitment to diligently seek Him increased dramatically as I began to realize how many times the Bible talks about "prisoners" and "captivity". I found out how many men God was able to use who were once murderers, adulterers, liars, thieves and reprobates. Many of them spent time as a prisoner. God has a way of showing His strength in man's weakness (II Cor. 12:9-10)!

I began to ignore all the remarks from unbelievers who did not want to change their lives or circumstances. The more time I spent seeking after God, the more hopeful, joyful and fulfilled I became. I refused parole and decided instead to discharge my sentence. The next twenty-two months seemed to fly by after I decided to treat my remaining months in prison like I was in "Bible College" or "Bible Boot Camp".

I know, in my case, that "Jail-House Religion" was "the real thing", not "a cheap imitation". The changes in me have been permanent, not temporary. In prison, I committed to spending significant, quality time seeking God daily, and I have continued this daily time with God since my release. I have never been disappointed in any way from my diligent pursuit of His wisdom, knowledge, understanding and truth (Heb. 11:6; Pr. 9:10; Psalm 1:1-3; Jn. 14:6). Now, instead of the oppressive emotional and heavy spiritual burdens I had carried for so long, the Holy Spirit within me has filled me with the incredible lightness of His fruit – more love, real joy, true peace, increased patience and self-control, etc. (Gal 5:22-25).

GOD'S FORGIVENESS

I was saved as a young boy in a Baptist church where my family attended. However, for most of my life I did not attend church or make any serious attempt to follow Jesus. As you now can imagine, there were many things I had done contrary to God. In the poor spiritual and emotional state I lived for so long prior to re-dedicating my life, I believed that I had "gone too far and done too much" for God to forgive me. I was overcome with guilt, regret, remorse and shame. Have you ever felt this way?

I read in a booklet by RBC Ministries, "The Forgiveness of God", that "If we believe our emotions, we may feel we have gone too far. Our self-contempt seems deserved. But there's hope. God wants us to believe in His ability to forgive sins we cannot forget." Our Heavenly Father is angry at sin, but "His anger is not a denial of His love...The truth is that His love is equal to His anger, and because of His love He found a way to show mercy." He sent His Son, Jesus.

It was great news to me when I learned that my sin was forgiven. My guilt was removed. By one Man, once and for all! "Because of the unlimited scope of Christ's death on the cross, we have received forgiveness not only for past sins, but for all sins – past, present, and future... The moment we trust Christ as Savior, we are given immunity from punishment. The issue is settled: Our case is closed and God will not open the files of our guilt again. Just as the courts of earth honor the principle of double jeopardy, heaven will not judge twice those whose sins have been punished in Christ. We will not be tried again for the sins He bore in our place."

Jesus was made sin with our sinfulness, so that we could be made righteous with His righteousness. The Father declares as righteous all those who appeal to the death of Christ as payment for their sin. No sin is excluded. We are saved by grace alone through faith alone in Jesus Christ alone. There is nothing in the entire universe more powerful than the Blood of Jesus that takes away our sin. When we do not deny the Spirit–and thereby accept by faith what Jesus did for us–there is no sin (and no sinner) beyond God's love and forgiveness.

My many sins were taken away! This was a "break-through" realization for me. I knew I could start over. I found present and eternal hope, and freedom in Jesus, when I accepted the Father's forgiveness! Have you finally and fully accepted His mercy, love and forgiveness?

FORGIVING MYSELF

After I truly accepted the Father's forgiveness, He began to show me the importance of forgiving myself, so that my past would stay in the past. That way, I could be unburdened of the guilt, shame, regret, remorse and embarrassment I had been carrying for so long. When I finally put my past behind me, I began to trust God one day at a time with my future (Phil. 3:13-14; Isaiah 43:18-19).

After I had been in prison long enough to be free of all the physical effects of my addictions, I began to think more clearly. I was honest with myself and God. I realized I hated myself for what I had done to ruin my life. I never blamed anyone else - only me - for the poor choices I made, one after another, that eventually led me to prison. I was angry at "me". I hated "me". In fact I could not even look at myself in the mirror as I was shaving or brushing my teeth because I was so disappointed for having foolishly wasted so much of my life, and for mis-using the talents God had given me.

I had broken relationships with, and pushed away, all my friends and family. Having been homeless for most of the three years leading up to my incarceration, I was left with no material possessions other than what was zipped-up inside a single, hanging garment bag in the prison's property room. And now I was a convicted sex offender. I was convinced there was no hope of anything ever getting better. I thought my future could never be any better than my past.

I will never forget the first glimmer of hope I experienced as I began to accept the Father's forgiveness of me and the removal of all my sin – past, present and future. I had never experienced the peace, emotional freedom and mental release I felt when He showed me I must forgive myself, so I could trust Him and move forward as the "new creature" He made me when I was "born again". I had to make a deliberate and determined choice to "let the past be the past".

It was clear to me that God had forgiven me, but I couldn't forgive myself. Did you ever feel this way?

One day I read something that made me think, "If the blood of Jesus was good enough for God the Father to forgive me, isn't it good enough for me to forgive myself? Who am I to require more than God does for forgiveness of sin? Am I better or more important than God?" Certainly not!

I finally realized there is absolutely nothing I could do about the past. Guilt, shame, regret, remorse and embarrassment had overwhelmed me for far too long. It had paralyzed me with fear, anxiety and depression, all of which kept me from moving forward. I was stuck. I decided that, more than anything else, I needed and wanted to trust God with my future.

I accepted the truth of His Word that He no longer held my past against me. He showed me I too had to stop holding my past against myself. I needed to accept His forgiveness, forgive myself, and move on. Are you stuck? Do you also need to forgive yourself?

GIVING AND RECEIVING FORGIVENESS

In my sin, I had in one way or another offended all my family and friends. I had pushed or driven everyone away. As I began to learn about forgiveness, I sensed that I needed to get past my pride so that I could humble myself to ask forgiveness from the ones I had offended who I could go ahead and contact from inside prison. At first, it was my two older brothers and my younger sister. I felt a burden begin to lift off of me as I wrote and mailed those first letters asking for forgiveness.

It was a great experience to hear my name called at "mail call" for the first time in the ten months that I had then been incarcerated. My two brothers quickly answered me, and let me know they were not holding anything against me. They both expressed their regret for where I was and why I was there, but they also both asked if they could do anything to help me.

God showed me that it might just be possible to receive forgiveness from others if I would just humbly ask.

With my sister, however, it took until after I had been released and walking out my Christian life for a time, before she forgave me. I had offended her the most. But, praise God, our relationship has been restored, and we are closer than we have been in a long time.

My son was the same way. In spite of the many letters I wrote him, he never responded while I was incarcerated. But in early 2013, two years after my release, God arranged a wonderful reunion meeting of reconciliation. What a blessing!

As I continued to study the Word during my incarceration, I also learned that I needed to forgive those who had offended and hurt me throughout my life. That was difficult at first, but I made a conscious decision to forgive them. All the bad feelings, and desire to get even, that I had been carrying was hurting only me. I decided to just give it all up and let it go.

What I discovered was that when we hold un-forgiveness towards someone, it causes a root of bitterness in us – a stronghold for the enemy. Like the unforgiving servant in Matthew 18:21-35, we turn ourselves over to "the tormenters" of anger, resentment, hatred, temper, and control – all of which can lead to retaliation, violence and even murder.

A "seed" of un-forgiveness planted in a "ground of hurt" gives us a "harvest" of pain. It grieves our spirit, torments our mind, and distresses us emotionally. All these, combined with a desire for vengeance or retaliation, hurt us–not the person who offended us. Often times they may not even realize their offense. This has been likened to drinking poison ourselves, thinking it will kill the other person! This is madness, and totally self-destructive.

One of the primary reasons Jesus came was so we could have forgiveness through His blood. One of the last things Jesus did was to cry out to God, asking His Father to forgive those who had spit upon Him, ridiculed Him, beat Him, mocked Him, and nailed Him to that cross. I'm sure he did not "feel" like forgiving them, yet that's what He chose to do, and prayed to His Father in like manner. We must also be willing to love and pray for those who have harmed us. We must be willing to forgive them. Aren't there people you too should choose to forgive?

FREEDOM FROM ADDICTIONS

Many people in "the free world" are in self-imposed, self-constructed prisons. Whether we are in an actual prison behind razor wire, or not, people everywhere struggle with "addictions" that negatively impact their lives–such as pride, selfishness, depression, anger, pornography, alcohol, prescription medicines, illegal drugs and many others. We may have been enslaved by them for many years. I know I was certainly in a prison of my own making many years before I was actually incarcerated.

Oftentimes, we indulge in addictive behavior to try to fill up the emptiness we feel inside and/or to avoid thinking about and dealing with the root causes of the addictions. At first, dealing with the underlying issues is emotionally painful, and our natural tendency is to avoid pain, even when something good like freedom awaits us on the other side. But the Word of God is clear that Jesus took all our pain, shame, guilt and sin on Himself when He hung on the Cross.

He took all our burdens on Himself so we could be free to live and walk in the abundantly blessed life He planned for us.

Most of us are familiar with the last part of John 8:31-32, "you shall know the truth and the truth will set you free". Almost all of us who have been incarcerated have seen it quoted in courtrooms. In actual fact, the truth did not set me free; rather it got me locked up!

I did not realize that the freedom promised as a result from knowing the truth is dependent on the verse preceding it regarding obedience to the teachings of Jesus. If we "hold" to His teaching we are true followers–the pre-condition for "knowing the truth". Who is the Truth? **Jesus** (John 14:6). So that means that to the extent we know, obey and follow Jesus, the truth of His teachings will set us free! This was truly a new revelation of what had always been a very familiar verse, even to a "heathen" like I once was.

As I studied this sometime after my release, the Spirit prompted me to meditate on how this applied to me. I had determined in 2009 to radically follow Jesus, and do my best to obey His teachings. Certainly I was growing in the knowledge of Him as "the Truth" as I studied His Word and spent quality time in His Presence daily. Consequently, for quite some time, I had in fact realized inside me a freedom I had never experienced before (accompanied by real joy and true peace). But as I thought deeper about this I asked myself, "What has the truth set me free from?"

The Spirit prompted me to make a list of oppressions, strongholds and addictions that I was once in bondage to, but from which I have now been set free. The list you saw earlier on page 39 of this booklet was the result. Believe me, like Paul, I was "the chief of sinners" – it is a very long list–and I add to it as the Spirit reveals. Why have I chosen to be this embarrassingly direct and transparent with you? Because I want you to know that if God can change me so miraculously inside and out, He can change anybody! Do you want to be forever finished with being a slave to old strongholds and addictions?

I am truly free of all those things and I have not been seriously tempted to return to any of them because I quickly take captive every "old man" thought the enemy brings. I know now that those thoughts and temptations the enemy throws at me daily all belong to the "old man" who is now "dead" (Romans 6:6-7). I am a new creature (II Cor. 5:17)! I do not let Satan convince me to resurrect that old, dead man! Therefore, I now experience daily the freedom and liberty of an abundant, over-flowing LIFE in Christ! I know who I am now in Him!

This is only accomplished by totally surrendering daily to the leadership of the Holy Spirit in my life. I am dead, and the life I live now is not me, but Christ living in me, by His Holy Spirit (see Gal. 2:20).

If God can save me and set me free (and He has), He can save anyone and free them from every form of bondage. Yes, this really does include you!

Jesus has liberated us to live an abundant life. Don't remain enslaved. Let Jesus set you free and choose to stay free!

THE KEY TO STAYING FREE

One of the most important things I had to learn in order to remain free from addictions, resist temptations and overcome depression was how to "take my thoughts captive to the obedience of Christ". See II Corinthians 10:3-5.

As Joyce Meyers described, the battlefield is in the mind! Sometimes it may seem we fight against impossible odds. The enemy wants you to believe it is always a battle, and it is always uphill. But I want you to know that God has already provided the victory and it is relatively easy to maintain it. Do you want to know the secret?

We often hear people say "resist the devil and he will flee" (James 4:7b), but many don't realize that the enemy does not have to flee if you don't first "submit to God" (James 4:7a); and then, after resisting the devil and his demons, we must "draw near to God so that God draws near to us" (James 4:8).

So the secret I have learned is to "submit to God" first as soon as I discern the enemy's attack when he tries to plant his deceitful lies and thoughts in my mind. By submitting first to God I can successfully recognize and resist the wrong thoughts, and take them captive by rejecting them and filling my mind instead with the thoughts of God.

How does one "submit to God"? By countering the lies, accusations and hopelessness of the enemy with the truth, acceptance and eternal hope of the Word of God. We must know what God says about us in His Word in order for us to successfully combat and take captive what the enemy says about us, or accuses us with. And when we confess God's Word about our situation we are able to "draw near to God". Doesn't this make good sense?

For example, we read in Luke 4:1-14, that Jesus Himself countered the enemy's temptations successfully when He came out of the wilderness by recognizing the devil's voice and responding to him with the Word of God. Note that the Word Jesus utilized was very specific to the area of temptation. Jesus knew what the Word said and used it to counter the enemy. We must do likewise.

(By the way, did you notice that Jesus was full of the Spirit, and led by the Spirit, in the wilderness; and, also was in the power of the Spirit coming out of the wilderness (Luke 4:1 and 4:14)? If Jesus had to have the Holy Spirit, so do we! As I will discuss later, the empowerment of the Holy Spirit is critical for us in every area of our walk in Christ. But I digress...)

So, what is the secret to knowing the truth disclosed in the Word of God regarding His thoughts about us as "new creations in Christ"? I believe the secret is to daily confess aloud what the Word of God says about us, and to pray personalized daily prayers to ask the Father to help us apply the Word to our lives in every situation.

Let me recommend something to you. While I was still incarcerated, two different ministers encouraged me to begin the practice of agreeing daily with God about what His Word says about me, and praying powerful, personalized daily prayers over my life. I typed these up after my release, and I am enclosing them near the end of this book for your review and use.

I encourage you to repeat these daily for six months, even if you only whisper loud enough where only you hear it. "Faith comes by hearing, and hearing by the Word of God" according to Romans 10:17. These daily confessions are so very powerful because they are all directly from the Word of God. And praying the Word of God is the most powerfully effective request of the Father that you could ever possibly pray!

We must know what God says about us so that we can recognize and reject the lies of the enemy, taking captive every thought to the obedience of Christ. I challenge you to confess and pray these daily for an extended period. After six months continue to recite them at least weekly thereafter. I promise you they will change the way you speak, think, pray and act.

REPENTANCE

Clearly, everything that happened in my life leading up to prison was not what God had planned and intended for me. Rather, it was the result of my slow, steady, downward spiral into utter depravity. See Romans 1:18-32. If your Bible had pictures in it, mine would be there, for this was certainly a picture of me.

God turned me over to my own perverted and misguided, selfish desires which led to a "reprobate" mind – one that can rationalize and do the most evil, despicable things and still convince itself that they are good and accept-able. I was "dead" – like a walking zombie – in my sin and self-deception.

Like the prodigal son (Luke 15:11-24), when I came to my senses in pris-on 10 months into my stay of 32 months, I was empty. I had a "longing" for something more than what I had available to me in my sin, my mess. I longed to "go home". The parable of the prodigal son really got my attention. I could really identify with him. He demonstrated for me that true repentance is "brokenness", and a change of life-direction.

I learned that repentance is not an emotion – for example, not the feeling of "I am sorry", or, "I feel bad about what I've done" – rather, it is a decision. It is like deciding to make a "U-turn" on a highway. You are then headed in the opposite direction from where you were going. Someone in true repentance does not just say "I'm sorry I did that"; they will also live a different life demonstrating a new mind-set of "I won't do it again".

The Greek words translated as "repentance" in the New Testament mean "to think differently", "to change your mind", "to turn about in opinion", "to turn about from an intended way"; and, Webster's Dic-tionary defines it as "to turn from sin and resolve to reform one's life".

In order for me to return to the Father, I had to go by way of repen-tance. True repentance is the only way to salvation in and through Jesus Christ. Has true repentance changed your direction? Have you made a "U-turn"?

JESUS CHRIST IS THE ONLY WAY - DO NOT BE DECEIVED!

When four of Jesus' closest disciples went to Him privately to ask Him what would be the signs of His Second Coming and of the "end of the age", Jesus warned them several times not to be deceived. Surely, we are even now seeing all the signs come to pass before our very eyes just as He foretold. Likewise, we are already seeing signs of the great deception.

I believe the greatest part of this deception is to try to convince the world that there are more ways to God and Heaven than just through Jesus. THAT IS A LIE. DO NOT BE DECEIVED. The only way to Father God is through the finished work of Jesus Christ of Nazareth at the cross and through His resurrection.

Many are suggesting that Jesus is just one way to Heaven, not necessarily the only way. This has reportedly come from even a few influential leaders within "Christian" circles! It is heresy to espouse this view.

In this age of secular humanism where mankind says they determine their own fate and future, not God, we as Christians are susceptible to their attempts to convince everyone that truth is "relative" to what is going on in society, and so it changes with the times. We are urged to be tolerant of everyone for every reason. No-one must be "offended". We are told that everyone must be "included" and not "confronted" in any way about anything.

While we must certainly treat those who do not agree with us with respect, kindness and gentleness, we must be very careful not to compromise on Who we know is Truth–the Son of God, Jesus Christ. Jesus makes it very clear that He is the only way, the only truth and the only life. He assures us that no-one gets to the Father except through Him (see John 14:6).

Peter preached about this truth about Jesus in Acts 4:12 when he said, "Salvation is found in no one else, for there is no other name under heaven given to mankind by which we must be saved." Isaiah quotes Jehovah, Father God, in Isaiah 43:11 as saying, "I, even I, am the Lord, and apart from me there is no savior."

I urge you to study carefully what Jesus revealed in Matthew 24, Mark 13, and Luke 21. Paul gives us further insight in 1 Thessalonians 4:13 – 5:11; 2 Thessalonians 2:1-17; 1 Timothy 4:1-2; and 2 Timothy 3:1-5. Read the visions of Daniel the prophet in Daniel chapters 7, 11 and 12. Of course, John tells us about the end of the age in Revelation. After studying these passages, I am certain you will agree that surely these times in which we are living are "the last days".

Brothers and Sisters, there is a sense of urgency in me to implore you to be careful you are not deceived – Jesus Christ of Nazareth is the only way to the Father in Heaven. Ask the Father for keen discernment through His Holy Spirit to recognize and avoid the coming great deception.

Jesus is coming back for His people (John 14:1-3).

He is coming quickly, in an instant of time (Matthew 24:27).

Jesus is coming soon, any day now (Revelation 22:12-13).

Are you sure you're ready (Matthew 24:42-44)???

HOLY SPIRIT EMPOWERMENT

When I was still incarcerated I saw several Christians who were released before me leave, only to return to prison within a year or so. I had also heard of others who had been following Jesus in prison with me that, after their release, fell away from their relationship with Jesus Christ and returned to "the world". I don't know if they returned to a physical prison, but they returned to their emotional and spiritual prisons from which they had once been set free. I know most of them had every good and honest intention to keep walking with Him, but many were powerless to resist old habits, places, and people.

Since I have been released, however, I know personally many former offenders who were transformed in prison, and who are still walking in Christ many years later. They are strong soldiers in God's army. I have seen God working in the lives of their families. I have seen them continue to prosper and experience the abundant life Jesus came to give us (John 10:10). Many have their own effective ministries now. Broken relationships have been restored. Broken hearts have been healed.

What makes the difference in these two groups of people? What made the difference with me? It was clearly the "baptism in the Holy Spirit". I firmly believe that the extra level of empowerment brought about by being baptized (immersed) in the Holy Spirit makes all the difference in enabling and empowering us to walk out our faith effectively and genuinely in prison and then, after our release, in "the free world".

When we accept the finished work of Jesus at the Cross, and confess His resurrection as the Son of God, the Holy Spirit comes to live in us. We "possess" the Spirit, and He begins His ongoing work of sanctification to steadily make our "new man" conform to the image of Christ. However, true empowerment – God's own power – comes to us, and for us, as we totally submit to the Holy Spirit and allow Him to "possess" us–one giant step more than us merely "possessing" Him inside us. We actually are able to allow Him to "possess" us!

We are baptized (immersed) into water as an outward representation of the inward change in us. We are buried with Christ in baptism (our "old man" died); and, we are raised to walk in newness of life (our "new man" came alive). But the Book of Acts makes it clear we should also desire to be baptized (immersed) into the Holy Spirit to receive the same power that resurrected Jesus from the dead – the power to walk out this new life in the way He desires for us. He in us, and us in Him!

We know the verse that says, "Greater is He that is in me than He that is in the world" (1 John 4:4). So, the Holy Spirit is in us. We possess Him. But another verse we know is "I can do all things through Him who strengthens me" (Phil. 4:13). That verse is also translated as, "I can do all things through the One who empowers me within". It is the Holy Spirit that empowers us within so that we can do everything the Father desires for us to do, and assigns us to do! But we must let Him do it. We must let Him possess us.

When Jesus finished His work on earth and returned to the Father, the Father sent the Holy Spirit to Earth for each of us. Jesus' followers at that time were instructed to wait until they were endued with power from on High before they began to carry out the ministry of Jesus. We should do likewise, that is, we should seek the power of the Holy Spirit before we move out among the people in the name of Jesus. We need the power of the Holy Spirit. Using only our own strength, we will burn out quickly, we will not be effective, and we can even do harm to His Kingdom.

Above all, we must remember the Holy Spirit is a person, He has a personality, and He can be grieved. His purpose in coming was to teach, lead, guide, correct, protect and comfort – the Helper who would walk alongside us as well as dwell within us. However, we must yield to Him and allow Him to do His work in us. If we refuse Him, resist Him, or grieve Him, we will restrict the work that the Father wants Him to do in our lives. He is a gift from the Father, and we need Him!

Paul depended upon the power of the Holy Spirit for his life and ministry. See, for example, Romans 15:17-19; II Corinthians 12:9; Ephesians 3:16-21; and, Colossians 1:29. In fact, Paul warned Timothy to stay away from religious people in the last days who deny the power of God, the Holy Spirit (see II Timothy 3:1-7).

Jesus needed the power of the Holy Spirit too! See Matthew 3:16-17; Matthew 4:1; Luke 4:1; Luke 4:14; Luke 4:18-19; and, Acts 10:38.

If Jesus, Paul and the other Apostles needed the Holy Spirit, surely we too must have all of God, the Holy Spirit, that He will give us! HE is the "game-changer" for our walk in the Christian life. I urge you to learn as much as you can about your Helper, Teacher, Counselor, Guide and Friend. Near the back of the book I am including more detailed information and scripture references about the Holy Spirit and His Baptism of fire and power. Would you study these prayerfully and deliberately?

We thank the Father for His gifts. He not only gave us His Son, Jesus, but He gave us His Holy Spirit. What a marvelous Father He is. When I think about it, I realize how gullible we are to believe the enemy's lie — the lie that the Holy Spirit is not for today, that we don't need Him. If anything, the truth is we need Him even more because we are living in the last of the last days when Scripture tells us that many will be deceived. The Holy Spirit can help us to not be deceived if we will let Him lead us, and recognize that we "host" Him as the very Presence of God in us. We need Him. We need Him in His fullness.

Have you asked the Father for Jesus to baptize you with the Holy Spirit (Luke 3:16)? If you ask the Father, He will give Him to you (Luke 11:13). Have you allowed the "rivers of living water" to flow from within you (John 7:38-39)? Our Father desires for us to walk in all His fullness by His Holy Spirit.

SURRENDER, SUBMISSION AND SANCTIFICATION

Before I was saved in prison I wanted to change my life but was powerless to do so. I learned that I could not change me. If I could've changed me I would have done so long before I was addicted, depressed, suicidal, homeless, lonely, lost, and eventually incarcerated! Is this also true of you? Have you tried to change yourself?

I tried to change myself an endless number of times but failed every time. So it was really great news to me that God did not expect me to change myself! Really. He only wanted me to allow His Holy Spirit to possess me, be willing daily to allow Him to lead me in the right way, and try my best to be instantly obedient to His promptings.

When we willingly surrender to God the Holy Spirit in us, and daily submit to be led by His Spirit instead of being led by our "flesh", He will begin His work of sanctification in us! Think about that. In other words, when we surrender to the Spirit, and submit to His leadership moment by moment, He will change us. We are not responsible for changing ourselves. Isn't that good news?

The best picture of submission is one of clay in a potter's hands. The potter transforms the clay from a shapeless handful of ugly mud into an exquisite object of beautiful art. The potter is totally in charge of the transformation, and the end product is determined in large part by his patience and skill. See Jeremiah 18:1-6; Isaiah 64:8; Romans 9:20-21.

As followers of Jesus, we can be sure we have the best Master Potter! The Father has sent us His Holy Spirit to accomplish this in us but we must cooperate fully with Him.

Sometimes God allows extreme circumstances, like prison or other hardships of life, to get our attention. Often these may come as a consequence of poor choices made by ourselves or others, but they are best viewed as opportunities for positive change. To be transformed, a piece of clay must be soft so it will yield. We must consciously and willingly submit to God the Holy Spirit.

Regardless of how bad a mess we have made of our lives, and how far we may have run away from God, we are never so broken or so lost that God cannot find us (Luke 15:4-7), joyfully accept our returning to Him (Luke 15:32), make us a new creation (II Corinthians 5:17) and establish His plan for our lives (Jeremiah 29:11-14).

However, we must be gratefully humble, prayerfully submissive and faithfully obedient. In humility we must recognize we cannot re-make ourselves and be grateful He can. In submission we must prayerfully put ourselves in His hands and patiently allow Him to form us, and subject us to the hardening fire of trials and circumstances. We must be always faithful in obedience to follow His instructions so that we will experience the best of His intentions as He accomplishes His will through us, forming us into the image of His Son (Romans 8:29).

The Word tells us that "His Divine Power has given us everything we need for life and godliness" (II Peter 1:3) and that He "teaches us to say 'No' to ungodliness and worldly passions, and to live self-controlled, upright and godly lives in this present age" (Titus 2:12). We must receive everything He has given us and be willing to say "No" to worldly temptations. He will help us if we let Him.

It is the sanctifying work of the Spirit that allows us to be obedient to Jesus Christ (1 Peter 1:2). As obedient children we are encouraged and empowered by His Holy Spirit not to "conform to the evil desires we once had when we lived in ignorance. But just as He who called you is holy, so be holy in all you do." (1 Peter 1:14-15). In our own strength this is impossible, but all things are possible with God the Holy Spirit doing the work of sanctification in us.

Near the back of this book I have included two prayers for submission I think you will find helpful. Pray them to the Father as you are led by His Holy Spirit. It is His job to change you. Your job is to willingly surrender, submit and be obedient to what He wants to do in His ongoing process of sanctification in you.

TRANSFORMATION

I am so thankful God impressed upon me to use those last 20 months of confinement as a time to grow spiritually in His Word and, thereby, to be "transformed by the renewing" of my mind (Rom. 12:1-2). I quit letting my "time do me" and started "doing my time". I quit watching TV and playing cards. Instead, the Spirit motivated me to spend that time in spiritual education and Christian life training programs sponsored by the Chaplain. Additionally, many Bible correspondence courses, frequent Chapel service attendance and intense personal Bible Study hours prepared a solid foundation for me and sowed seed in fertile ground.

I am now a living witness of the Father's grace, mercy, forgiveness and power in Christ Jesus. The Holy Spirit has never been more real to me. The differences in me are real and permanent. God has changed me from the inside out. My attitudes, thoughts, desires and speech have all drastically changed. I am truly a "new creature in Christ – old things are passed away, everything has been made new" (II Cor. 5:17).

After having now experienced the fullness, love, joy and peace of God in Christ Jesus, it is absolutely unthinkable that I would ever again be lured by Satan back into the emptiness, self-hate, anxiety and depression of that "old man" and his addictions. Truly, the Father's love and abiding presence of His Holy Spirit have worked a life-saving miracle in me through Jesus Christ! You can be certain He can do the same for you.

DO YOUR TIME WISELY

I am often asked what kinds of things I did in prison after I got saved but before I went home. As I stated earlier, I planned out every day as to how I could pursue more of God during my waking hours. I tried to separate myself as best I could from all the worldly activities going on around me such as watching TV, reading newspapers, playing cards, and the usual kinds of conversations most inmates have in prison. I'm certain you know what I'm talking about.

There was a verse I remember that really got my attention and I tried to apply it to my situation: "Be very careful, then, how you live-- not as unwise but as wise, making the most of every opportunity, because the days are evil. Therefore, do not be foolish, but understand what the Lord's will is." (Ephesians 5:15-17). We all know how much evil there is around us, especially in prison. God's will is for us to separate ourselves from it, and use our time wisely in living for Him.

I tried to focus as much as possible on studying the Word, memorizing scripture verses, and attending every sort of Chaplaincy class and almost every Christian worship service available to me. I completed many Correspondence Bible Study courses, and for one of them I earned a Study Bible for satisfactorily completing the course. What a wealth of information it contained in its verse commentaries, articles, concordance, subject index and maps!

While you are still incarcerated, for however brief or lengthy a time that may be, make a decision now to use your time wisely. Further your education. Study the Word and learn how to apply it to your daily life. Seek the Father diligently with all your heart. Cultivate an intimate, personal relationship with the Father through His Holy Spirit living in you. Choose to be led by the Spirit moment by moment, instead of being constantly influenced by fleshly desires, the world, or the devil and his demonic hosts.

The Holy Spirit is your teacher. He will help you. Pray often for wisdom, knowledge, understanding, truth, revelation, discernment, and how to apply them to your life. These are all things God wants you to have so He will give them if you ask. He has a plan and a hope-filled future for you.

God wants to use you right where you are. Many people tell me they want to "do prison ministry" when they are released. But I tell them that the most important person in prison ministry is the turned-on, committed Christian still locked up. That is the person who can see firsthand who needs help, who needs prayer, who needs encouragement – right there on the inside. In fact, I believe if you are not already engaging in prison ministry on the inside, you won't do it effectively, if at all, on the outside.

You should become a prayer warrior by praying boldly and diligently for the lost souls around you, for the officers in your unit, for the facility's administration, and for your family. In fact, praying for your family is one of the most powerful and beneficial gifts you can give them. As I learned to pray inside prison I saw the Lord move in mighty ways that built my faith and made me want to pray more!

If your unit offers a faith-based housing area, apply for it. Attend every sort of Chaplaincy program and service that is offered. Read as many Christian books as possible. If your facility offers a spiritual mentorship program, apply for that too. Volunteer for your Chaplain. Get involved with the inside church.

Don't expect perfection from anyone in the church. Just do the best you can to walk your talk (1 Peter 2:11-12). As you know, people are watching, and wanting to know if your commitment is real. In fact, many privately hope it is real because it would mean more hope for them that they too could be changed by a real encounter with our living Lord Jesus.

If you mess up, get up, confess your sin to the Father (1 John 1:9), and keep headed in the right direction. Pay no attention to snide remarks from others. At judgment day, you will be standing in front of the King alone. Focus on pleasing Him daily instead of pleasing others. Make wise use of your time. You will be glad you did!

GOING HOME

As you look forward to the day you will be released, if you are like me you may wonder if you can really follow Christ out there "in the free world". You can. But it will require daily focus and commitment.

If I were to name nine most important things to help you be consistent and faithful about your commitment to follow Christ in "the free world", they would be:

1. Join a church and attend as often as possible.

2. Restore broken relationships–and work at maintaining them once restored.

3. Separate totally and permanently from the former bad influences of certain people, places and things.

4. Faithfully maintain prayer, Bible study and private worship daily.

5. Maintain a constant, prayerful attitude of gratefulness and humility towards God.

6. Get an accountability partner and meet regularly. Having a trusted accountability partner is an important factor in maintaining a faithful walk. It is very hard to try to do it alone.

7. Get actively involved in serving in an anointed ministry as a volunteer. As you invest yourself in the issues and challenges of others, the joy of the Lord will strengthen and enrich you. You will be drawn closer to the Father by the Holy Spirit, and your personal testimony will encourage others.

8. If you fall, quickly confess and truly repent. Get right back up on your Christian walk.

9. Forgive yourself. You did your time – put the past behind you and move on! You are a new creation (II Cor. 5:17)!!

HIS CALL ON MY LIFE

God has called me to minister to His lost and forgotten children – inmates, ex-cons, homeless, bi-polar, those who are depressed, addicts and sex offenders. Since I am now, or have recently been, "classified" as each one of these, the Father is using my experiences to reach others like me for the Kingdom. I answered God's call on my life to be an ordained and licensed servant of the Lord on February 23, 2012.

Today, my passion and reason for living is to let "the least of these" know the true and eternal freedom available by grace alone through faith alone in Jesus Christ alone.

I pray the Holy Spirit continues to work through me to bring the hope, love and grace of Jesus to many who are unloved, lost, hurting, forgotten, needy, despised, depressed and forsaken – people who are even now just like I once was.

I am humbly and eternally grateful for another chance to start over! He is not the God of second chances; rather, He is the God of another chance. His unlimited love, grace and mercy are always available to anyone who comes to Him in humility and sincerity. He gives us an unlimited number of chances.

My feelings are like those of Paul when he wrote to Timothy nearly 2,000 years ago:

> "I thank Christ Jesus our Lord, who has given me strength, that He considered me faithful, appointing me to His service. Even though I was once a blasphemer and a persecutor and a violent man, I was shown mercy because I acted in ignorance and unbelief. The grace of our Lord was poured out on me abundantly, along with the faith and love that are in Christ Jesus. Here is a trustworthy saying that deserves full acceptance: Christ Jesus came into the world to save sinners – of whom I am the worst. But for that very reason I was shown mercy so that in me, the worst of sinners, Christ Jesus might display His unlimited patience as an example for those who would believe on Him and receive eternal life. Now to the King eternal, immortal, invisible, the only God, be honor and glory for ever and ever. Amen."

(1 Timothy 1:12-17)

In sincerity, truth and love I am, and will remain, a humble, grateful child of our Father, and a radical follower of the Lord Jesus Christ, by His Holy Spirit in me!

P.S. – Perhaps I should consider changing the title of this testimony to:

"From Park Avenue... to Park Bench...to Prison

...to Preacher!"

WHAT DO I
NEED TO DO?

YOU CAN HAVE "THE REAL THING"

"The Real Thing" has nothing to do with "religion."

Rather, it is an intimate personal relationship with our Heavenly Father, because of the finished work of Jesus at the Cross. The Holy Spirit comes and seals us as His very own, and begins an ongoing work in us to conform us to the image of Christ Jesus.

You can begin this exciting and abundant life today. It will continue throughout all eternity.

First, acknowledge and confess that you have sinned against God.

Second, renounce your sins – determine that you are not going back to them. Turn away from sin. Turn to God.

Third, by faith receive Christ into your heart. Surrender your life completely to Him. He will come to live in your heart by the Holy Spirit.

You can do this right now.

Start by simply talking to God. You can pray a prayer like this:

"Oh God, I am a sinner. I'm sorry for my sin. I want to turn from my sin. Please forgive me. I believe Jesus Christ is Your Son; I believe He died on the Cross for my sin and You raised Him to life. I want to trust Him as my Savior and follow Him as my Lord from this day forward, forevermore. Lord Jesus, I put my trust in You and surrender my life to You. Please come into my life and fill me with your Holy Spirit. In Jesus' Name. Amen."

If you just said this prayer, and you meant it with all your heart, we believe you just got Saved and are now Born Again in Christ Jesus as a totally new person.

"Therefore, if anyone is in Christ, he is a new creation; the old has gone, the new has come!" (II Corinthians 5:17)

We urge you to go "all in and all out for the All in All"! (Pastor Mark Batterson, *All In*)

We suggest you follow the Lord in water baptism at your earliest opportunity. Water baptism is an outward symbol of the inward change that follows your salvation and re-birth.

The grace of God Himself gives you the desire and ability to surrender completely to the Holy Spirit's work in and through you (Philippians 2:13).

The Baptism in the Holy Spirit is His empowerment for you.

YOU CAN RECEIVE THE BAPTISM IN THE HOLY SPIRIT

The Baptism in the Holy Spirit is a separate experience and a Holy privilege granted to those who ask. This is God's own power to enable you to live an abundant, overcoming life. The Bible says it is the same power that raised Jesus from the dead (Romans 1:4; 8:11; II Cor. 4:13-14; 1 Peter 3:18).

Have you asked the Father for Jesus to baptize you (immerse you) in the Holy Spirit (Luke 3:16)? If you ask the Father, He will give Him to you (Luke 11:13). Have you allowed the "rivers of living water" to flow from within you (John 7:38-39)? Our Father desires for us to walk in all His fullness by His Holy Spirit.

The power to witness, and live your life the way Jesus did in intimate relationship with the Father, comes from asking Jesus to baptize you in the Holy Spirit. To receive this baptism, pray along these lines:

Abba Father and my Lord Jesus,

Thank you for giving me your Spirit to live inside me. I am saved by grace through faith in Jesus. I ask you now to baptize me in the Holy

Ghost with Your fire and power. I fully receive it through faith just like I did my salvation. Now, Holy Spirit, come and rise up within me as I praise God! Fill me up Jesus! I fully expect to receive my prayer language as You give me utterance. In Jesus' Name. Amen.

Now, out loud, begin to praise and glorify JESUS, because He is the baptizer of the Holy Spirit! From deep in your spirit, tell Him, "I love you, I thank you, I praise you, Jesus."

Repeat this as you feel joy and gratefulness bubble up from deep inside you. Speak those words and syllables you receive – not in your own language, but the heavenly language given to you by the Holy Spirit. Allow this joy to come out of you in syllables of a language your own mind does not already know. That will be your prayer language the Spirit will use through you when you don't know how to pray (Romans 8:26-28). It is not the "gift of tongues" for public use, therefore it does not require a public interpretation.

You have to surrender and use your own vocal chords to verbally express your new prayer language. The Holy Spirit is a gentleman. He will not force you to speak. Don't be concerned with how it sounds. It is a heavenly language!

Worship Him! Praise Him! Use your heavenly language by praying in the Spirit every day! Paul urges us to "pray in the Spirit on all occasions with all kinds of prayers and requests." (Ephesians 6:18)

CONTACT US

We would love to hear your feedback or answer your questions.

- We would especially like to know if you made a decision to receive Jesus into your heart and prayed the prayer of Salvation on page 88 Or maybe you had prayed a similar prayer before, but this is the first time you really meant it from your heart. Tell us about your decision.

- Perhaps you made a decision to rededicate your life to Christ – to go "all in and all out" for Jesus! If so, we would like to know so we can encourage you. Please write to us.

- If you prayed the prayer to ask Jesus to baptize you in the Holy Spirit, please tell us.

As a further aid and encouragement, we would like to teach you more about how to follow Jesus – how to be a true disciple. A disciple is a "disciplined learner" and we want to share many truths with you about how to have an intimate relationship with God the Father, by the Holy

Spirit. Jesus came to reconcile us to the Father. We want to help you develop a meaningful relationship with Him.

Please ask us to include you in our Discipleship Program whereby you will receive an encouraging teaching every two months or so. This is not the kind of lesson you are required to fill in and send back to us. You must only desire to be encouraged regularly in the Lord, and be willing to prayerfully study the materials. That's all.

Please send your comments, questions and feedback to:
Freedom in Jesus Prison Ministries
Attn: Stephen – LNM
P.O. Box 939
Levelland, TX 79336

Be sure to plainly print your full name, I.D. number, full name of facility, and your complete mailing address.

Ask your loved ones to check out our ministry website:
www.fijm.org
They can learn more about Stephen Canup's books at
www.stephencanup.com

We pray you are blessed abundantly by our Father every day, in every way, in Christ Jesus as you seek Him daily in and by the Holy Spirit!

I CHALLENGE YOU!!!

G od is able to transform your life in the same way He did the four
men in this book.

But you must understand that He rewards those who diligently and
earnestly seek Him (Hebrews 11:6); and, that you are transformed by
renewing your mind through applying the principles in His Word to
your daily life (Romans 12:1-2).

I challenge you to:

- Start every day with the Word and the Spirit. Ask the Holy Spirit to
  help you apply His Truth to your life. Let the Spirit use the Word
  to transform you.

- Look up every scripture reference in this book. Mark the verses in
  your own Bible. Memorize the ones that mean the most to you.

- Study the scriptural principles in this book in small groups. Sharing
  concepts from the Word with others helps you learn and apply them
  to your life.

- Show this book to others. As an ambassador for Christ (see II Corinthians 5:18-20), please use this book as a tool to reach the lost and encourage the Body of Believers. After sharing it with them, encourage them then to contact me to request their own copy of the book so they can study it and loan it to others. Each person who wants one must write me individually because I can only send one book to each person.

- Pray daily for us and for our ministry. We need your prayers.

- Do you want to help us continue to provide books like these free to prisoners? At your first opportunity, begin a program of regular giving to us so we can better minister to others who want to be free from every form of bondage. Former prisoners helping prisoners is what we are all about.

REAL QUESTIONS FROM

PRISONERS WITH HONEST ANSWERS

FROM FORMER LEPERS

Were you released from prison on parole? Did you wear a monitor?

STEPHEN:

No, I was not on parole when I was released from prison on December 29, 2010. I had refused parole when it was offered in February, 2010, so I could "discharge" my sentence and thereby be free of standard parole requirements after release. In effect, in my case, I only had to serve ten months longer in prison in order to be free of two years on parole. Since I was not on parole, I did not have to wear a monitor after I was released.

I served my time in Tennessee where I had three, two-year sentences stacked, so the term of my sentence was for a total of six years. In Tennessee, at the time, an inmate received two days off his sentence for every one day served. In addition, an inmate could earn "good time" credit of approximately 10%, if I remember correctly. Therefore, I was able to fully discharge the six-year sentence in about 32 months.

Why did I decide to discharge my sentence? I already knew something of what it was like to be on a monitor, and under supervision by the

State of Tennessee, because originally in 2007 I had received probation instead of being sent to prison. But having been diagnosed as bi-polar about 15 years earlier, and living pretty much in a constant state of severe hopelessness and depression (before I was "saved" in prison in 2009), I didn't really even try to meet the terms of my probation.

I was so ashamed of myself for my many poor decisions that I pretty much gave up. Since I was on the monitor in late 2007 and early 2008, they knew where I was when I quit reporting. I lived in the worst state of suicidal depression I had ever experienced. I did not try to run, hide or cut off my monitor. I just never reported. I also failed to do my required annual update of the sex offender registry in March, 2008. Finally, in May, 2008, they came with a warrant to the Nashville Rescue Mission where I had been since November, 2007.

Another reason I denied parole was that God was teaching me so much from His Word in prison after I gave Him my life in early 2009 and went "all in" for Jesus. When offered parole in early 2010, I did not feel I was ready to be out and stay out. Also, I did not have anyone waiting for me to get out that really needed me.

I wanted to be as prepared spiritually as I could be, and I wanted to give the Holy Spirit a little more time in His ongoing process of sanctification of my soul, so I decided my physical body could wait a little longer to be free. My spirit and soul were already experiencing freedom even behind razor wire.

I realize many prisoners have longer sentences than I did, so staying in prison longer in order to discharge their sentence may not be practical, or even possible. Everyone has different circumstances, and some states may have different requirements than Tennessee where I was incarcerated. My advice is to seriously seek the Lord's will and Holy Spirit guidance before making any decisions for yourself after carefully considering your unique circumstances.

BRANDON:

Yes to both questions. I was released from prison on September 17, 2019, after serving twelve years and nine months. That left me with eight years and three months to do on parole in order to complete my 21-year sentence.

I was released with a leg monitor which was part of my parole stipulations. When I received my parole answer it stated I would be placed on a leg monitor for six months. Before I left the Huntsville Unit the monitor was attached to my ankle. In reviewing the paperwork with the woman who placed the monitor on me, I was informed that I would have to complete a whole year before it's removal would even be considered, which was a complete surprise to me. After fourteen months on the monitor, I was told that it would remain in place until I am re-considered in September, 2021.

DUANE:

I was released on Parole. I will be on some sort of supervision for the rest of my life, I suppose. I wear a monitor and I am under the SISP (Super intensive Supervision Program), which means that I have to make a schedule and have it approved by my parole officer. I am restricted to only those activities I need to do, not what I want to do. My parole officer decides what I need to do. I will be wearing this monitor for at least a year, but I know of people who are on their monitor for more than one year. At the end of a year, I will be evaluated and the decision will be made whether I can come off my monitor or not. Sometimes it seems like I have not really left prison at all, but all I have to do is walk outside and look around to see the lie of that. No matter how restrictive my supervision seems, it is a million times better than being behind bars.

Wearing a monitor is a stressful and fearful thing. In the Fall of 2020 they changed out my equipment to a better system that had caused problems for everyone. I especially have had problems because, unlike all the other people involved, I am the one who will go back to prison if things go wrong. And go wrong they do, on December 30 I got up to begin my day and my monitor simply fell off. I am writing this as I await being contacted by my Parole officers. I am very fearful and anxious about how this is going to turn out. Being sent back to prison because the State has to use equipment supplied by the cheapest bidder is not how I envisioned things going for me. I am also afraid how this will affect my job, as my employer is frustrated by my situation as well. Being on parole is alot like being in prison; the other people in my life, family, friends, employers; they are all on parole with me. They experience and suffer the same things I do. This is something I must endure, and I am able to get through this only because I have the support of those same family members, friends, and even my employer who are going through this with me.

Thankfully, they believed the truth about how my monitor came off and did not send me back to prison. Praise God!

RUSSELL:

Yes, I was; they placed the monitor on me when I was at the Walls Unit immediately prior to my release. I thought I would be on it for at least a year. During that time, I was required to make a schedule with parole if I wanted to go anywhere outside of my parole address, which was Kingdom Towers in Lubbock, TX. But, to my surprise, my parole officer removed my monitor after only sixty days. Once again, God provided a huge blessing for me by removing the monitor so quickly!

How were you able to leave the state where you were incarcerated? Can you move into another city or state while on parole?

STEPHEN:

Since I discharged my sentence, and therefore was not on parole, my main first requirement was that I had to go to the Davidson County Metro Police Department in Nashville, TN, to update the sex offender registry from before I was taken to prison.

My family was willing to help me start over in Texas, praise God! They had been in the process of making arrangements for about two months before my release, and had already informed the City of Levelland, TX, Police Department that I was wanting to move there. So, after I related all this to the Police Officer in Nashville, he contacted the Levelland Police Officer in charge of the sex offender registry to inform them they were letting me leave the State of Tennessee, and transferring my sex offender registry requirements to Texas.

They gave me a certain length of time to get to Levelland, TX, and check in with the Police Department. I think it was only three to five days, but I do not remember exactly, but as soon as I arrived there I went to check-in and fill out the Texas Registry paperwork with the Levelland Police Department.

If you are on parole and want to leave the state, there are other requirements. Although I did not do any research on this because I was not on parole, my understanding is that someone on parole would have the added duty and requirement to apply for approval under the Interstate Compact. Of course, they would have to also have the approval and coordination of their parole officer.

Done properly, I do not personally know of any reason why a parolee, including a registered sex offender, cannot apply to leave their current state (or city) if the other state and city agree to it in advance, and they work together to coordinate the exact timing of departure and arrival. Of course, everything must be approved in advance through the parole office.

BRANDON:

Once I was released on parole I remained in the State of Texas. While on parole, there is nothing in particular preventing the parolee from moving to another state as long as the parolee gets permission from both states and follows each state's guidelines. Your parole officer should be able to help you investigate the possibilities and perhaps guide you through the process.

DUANE:

I was not able to leave Texas. I wanted to go home in another state, but the health concerns of my Father and the Covid 19 pandemic led the parole officer back home to deny my application. My charges and parole stipulations may have played a part in this decision, but this was not presented as the reason for my denial. I could probably move back home now that I have been released, but I have not yet tried to do so. I have more support here now than I could receive back home and I have come to believe that it is not always a good thing to return to the old stomping grounds.

RUSSELL:

I did not leave the State of my incarceration.

How hard is it to find a job? How is the best way to disclose your criminal history? Can an ex-convict, a former felon or a former sex offender own their own business? What can I do while still incarcerated that will help me find work when I am released?

STEPHEN:

When I was released from prison I was almost 59 years old. Because I eventually wanted to go into prison ministry full-time, my two older brothers gave me enough monthly financial support to get by until I could claim early retirement on Social Security at age 62. My mentor and accountability partner, Don Castleberry, allowed me to start volunteering with Freedom in Jesus Ministries after I had been out and under his mentorship for about three months.

At the time, I was primarily doing computer and clerical tasks associated with starting our Correspondence ministry. Every now and then the ministry was able to pay me a few hundred dollars, but for the most part, I was a full-time volunteer. After about three years, I became Executive Director, and five years later, in 2020, I was named President.

For about five years the ministry has been able to pay a small salary. By this, God has enabled me to supplement my monthly social security payments, which because of my previous successful career, are pretty decent considering I was able to start collecting them at age 62.

I relate this to you to let you know, in my case, I never really had to look for another job. However, I have counseled many felons, including former sex offenders, as to how to approach looking for jobs after their release from prison. Furthermore, because I am very closely involved with Kingdom Towers, a Christian Residential Transitional Program with a capacity of 86 men, I am regularly informed about the success of men with a criminal record looking for jobs.

Some of the men who live there are former sex offenders whose charges involved adults. Unfortunately, there is a Day Care too close to the facility thereby prohibiting Kingdom Towers from housing former sex offenders whose charges involved a minor.

There are many employers who will give a felon an opportunity to prove themselves, including former sex offenders. Admittedly, it is sometimes a little harder for former sex offenders due to various reasons. Let me assure you that I know many felons, ex-convicts, and former sex offenders and all of them are working, so it is not impossible to find a job. God can open doors no man can close, and close doors no man can open! God has a plan and a job for you so trust Him to show you the way.

We encourage people to register with employment agencies as soon as they are released, especially those where employers regularly seek temporary workers. Getting hired for one of those jobs can be the best way to prove yourself. Showing up on time every day with a good attitude and working hard during the day will make a positive impression on any employer.

For every job interview, be completely honest about your past, but let them know that you have learned your lessons, done your time, and are not at all the person you used to be before prison. Emphasize your strengths, what skills and experience you had before, and how your time in prison has prepared you to be a good employee. They will almost always run a criminal background check so by being forthright and honest, you may be able to make a good impression over other people who are trying to hide their past. God always honors honesty, and potential employers do too.

I often recommend to former sex offenders to begin to develop skills they can use in their own small business. They may not always want to work for someone else. Rather than being at the mercy of employers who may not be as open to former sex offenders as they are other felons, being able to utilize your own skills to find and perform jobs as a self-employed person can be very satisfying. There are no reasons I know of that a former sex offender cannot own their own business unless that particular business requires a license from the State or city that is not normally granted to felons. Certainly, discretion and common sense are important in evaluating where a former sex offender may be working, self-employed or not.

In general, construction trades, painting, welding, landscaping or lawn care, agriculture, factory work, warehouse work, heating and air conditioning, plumbing, truck-driving, and similar areas are often "felon-friendly", even with former sex offenders. Whatever you can learn while still incarcerated that can develop your knowledge and experience in any of these areas is important. If you do not have a high school diploma, by all means, try to achieve your G.E.D. while you are incarcerated. Vocational training in prison can be very helpful to have on your job applications when you are released. Additional advanced education to achieve an Associates or Bachelor's degree can be very helpful too.

BRANDON:

For me it wasn't hard to find a job. After my release I kept my focus on God in a major way and things seemed to come to me. I know this sounds like a cliché but it is so true. Within a month I had two jobs. My parole address was approved for a Christian Residential Transition Program called Kingdom Towers in Lubbock, TX. God provided aid in all areas during and after my release.

There were many job interviews that came with a lot of "no" answers at the end, but I trusted God to do what only He could do, and He did! I interviewed at a construction company and I was able to tell them openly and honestly about my charges and my testimony about being saved. I was hired!

God gave me so much favor with the owner of the company that on my first day of work I rode around with him. He also took me shopping buying me all the things I would need for the job including a coat, under armor, shirts, pants and gloves. He most definitely was a God-send for me.

I suggest being open and honest about your charges. Most people respect the honest approach. That being said, before you share your past mistakes let your potential employer know some of your positive qualities, changes and accomplishments you have made since your charges.

Regarding the last question above, I know how important it is to use the time of incarceration to grow closer to God and to better yourself through education and learning trades and skills. These will add value to your skill set and potentially increase your ability to become the answer to someone's need.

I know of a man who served thirteen years in TDCJ. He was released and now has his own business sewing customized masks and other clothing items. There are other men that I know that have started their own businesses who were sex offenders, but personally I do not have any experience in that area.

DUANE:

I had no problem finding a job. My first employer placed some restrictions on me because of my criminal history, but he did not restrict my ability to work because of it. There are many companies that will not hire ex-felons, sex offenders, persons with drug charges, etc. It depends on the employer and what their company policy is. I do know that the first business I applied to hired me, and that all of the men here at Kingdom Towers who want to work have had no trouble finding work. I would caution you to be aware that there are a lot of employers who hire ex-felons because they are willing to work for less, but I have not experienced this.

When and what to disclose about your criminal history is a personal decision. I bring it right out front. That way if it is going to be a problem, I don't waste any more time than necessary to get it cleared up. I have been counseled that this is not the best way to handle my criminal history, but I firmly believe that it is. Some counsel that it is best to not bring it up until it comes up, but this may not occur until later in the relationship, whether it is at the workplace or in your personal life, and may cause problems. I would rather avoid any issues about what effect my criminal history may have on the relationship and the stress that comes with worrying about it. I recently obtained a better job with more hours. And again I was forthright early in the application process.

I know several former inmates who are self-employed, but have not yet met any who own a storefront type of business. I know of no reason why you could not do this, but I do know that some licenses are more difficult to obtain and some are beyond our reach as felons. My sexual criminal history will obviously play a part in any major life decision that involves the authorities and may have an adverse effect on whether or not I am permitted to do certain things. But I do not intend to let this keep me from trying if I ever want to open a business somewhere.

While you are incarcerated, get your issues resolved. Turn your life away from the attitudes, beliefs and behaviors that got you sent to prison. There are programs in prison that will help you begin to address any issues you may need to resolve, and to develop job skills while in prison; take advantage of them. You can also seek similar employment on your camp that will give you some exposure to the type of work environment that you wish to enter. Stay active in the prison work-force and develop habits that will help you to bring some positive, constructive contribution to a job.

Seek a relationship with Christ. Ask Him to dwell in you and guide you. When He leads you in a direction, follow. He will lead you to where you are to be in His Will. Or not. I did nothing, really, and He still reached out to me time after time. I really could have avoided a lot of grief if I had gotten the message earlier, but hindsight is always 20/20, and I would not be as sure as I am that I have found the Way.

RUSSELL:

Certainly it can be difficult to find a job as a former sex offender; but with God, anything is possible! My parole address is Kingdom Towers in Lubbock, TX which is a Christian Residential Transition Program for men. They are allowed to house sex offenders whose charges did not involve someone under eighteen or child pornography. There is a day care too close to the facility so the city makes them exclude anyone whose sex crime involved a minor. Their success rate for their residents is great; and, the facility already has a good reputation of turning out strong, good men in the Lord.

Your walk with God carries over into your daily life, 100%! If you are all in for God, He is all in for you. I can attest to that myself! I give God all the Glory because He provides for me every day! I own my own business and run it myself. I clean houses for a living, primarily for Realtors, and I try to always make sure the work is immaculate. In fact, I named the business "Rusty's Immaculate Cleaning Service."

My advice for interviews is to be up front and honest. Tell them you are not the person you used to be and that you are the person they need because no-one else will make them happier. Sell yourself and be confidant, it goes a long way!

While you are still incarcerated, actively look for whatever opportunities there are to gain trade skills, improve your education, increasing social and parenting skills, etc. As opportunities come up, take them. The main thing is don't be scared about the perception of your crime. Come out with your sleeves rolled up ready to face each day walking in the Lord and God will provide!

I know God forgives, but how do you handle living with the label the world puts on you as "an ex-convict", "a felon" or "a sex offender"? How do I keep from condemning myself and thinking of myself the same way the world does? How do you keep from being overwhelmed with memories of your past?

STEPHEN:

This may be the hardest challenge we face when we make a decision to follow Jesus and go "all in" for Him. The Word and the Holy Spirit work together after we become "a new creation" in Christ to help us bury "our old man".

Someone has said, "You must bury your past or it will bury you!" In our new walk with Christ Jesus, we must learn to listen to what God says about us instead of what the world says. They are only talking about my old man when they bring up my past, and he is dead. I refuse to let the enemy talk me into resurrecting him! I am a new man in Christ Jesus!

How do we apply this practically to our daily lives? First, we must daily re-commit to trying to please God and not men. This world is no longer our home. The Bible says we are just passing through on our way to our eternal home in Heaven. We should make it a habit to live every day with eternity uppermost in our mind. All the things that used to matter to us in our old life pale in significance to the things that matter to us now in the Kingdom of God.

Second, we must truly believe and receive the Truth that God the Father fully forgave us the moment we repented of our old lifestyle, deeds and words. He is not holding our past against us! The Blood of Jesus was fully applied to our sin, and because of that fact, when God the Father sees us He no longer sees the person we once were. We must be determined to see ourselves as the new person and fully receive the Truth of the power of the Blood of Jesus to wash away our sins.

Third, we must forgive ourselves and stop holding our past against ourselves. We must not fall for the enemy's accusations that keep us buried in guilt, shame, remorse and embarrassment over our past. When the enemy tries to bring up my past, out of my own mouth I enjoy turning to God and thanking Him that I am totally forgiven, set free, and brought out of darkness into His marvelous Light! When we "submit to God" we very effectively "resist the devil" and he "has to flee" (see James 4:7-8).

Fourth, we must choose to forgive others for everything that was ever done against us. Although we will probably never forget the worst things ever done to us, we still must choose to forgive. The Bible makes it clear that we must forgive others in order for us to be forgiven by the Father. Whatever was done to us is so much less than what was done to our Savior, Jesus; yet, He chose to forgive them even as Hung on the Cross. It was by and through the Cross that we are forgiven, and the Bible says as we have been forgiven, we must forgive others.

Fifth, we must learn to take every thought captive that is contrary to the truth and principles of Jesus Christ. That is, we must recognize the wrong thoughts from the world, the flesh and the devil and reject those quickly. As we progressively fill our mind and heart with the Word of God, the Holy Spirit will teach us to discern between the thoughts of God toward us versus the wrong thoughts from the world, the flesh and the devil.

In my longer testimony earlier in this book, "From Park Avenue... to Park Bench... to Prison", I share more information and many scriptures about how to be free from the world's labels; and, from the guilt, shame and remorse associated with our old way of living. I hope you will carefully study and apply what the Holy Spirit has been showing me since my release. What He has done for me, He will do for you.

BRANDON:

Instead of answering these questions individually, I am going to sum all this up in one. The answer is in 2 Corinthians 5:16-21. It's simply realizing how the Lord has made a way to de-program us from the labels that have been put on us through society or our past. This can be an inner battle (Genesis 32:22-32) that can only be won through relationship with God. The more time we spend with our Creator the more we learn about Him and ourselves. We learn who we are in Him and through Him – who we truly are!

Once we know this we can walk in boldness and courage rather than in self-condemnation or self-pity based on people's labels. We know who we are, but more importantly Whose we are. We align our identity to God's Word and live and walk it out. Ultimately it comes down to whether we will believe men or the devil over God; and we all know the devil is a liar and the father of lies. As for the memories of my past, I'm too focused on my present, and the future God has for me to become overwhelmed with my past.

Remember Joseph, the first falsely accused sex offender in the Bible? After Joseph stepped into his leadership role in Egypt, he named his first born son Manasseh signifying how God had made him forget all the toil, hurt and pain of his past (Genesis 41:51). Something you might think would destroy you or hold you back is the very thing God can use to promote you, and make it seem like nothing once you step into the life God has for you. The past can be a tool to remind us of God's faithfulness and our progress in God's process for our lives. Consciously choose to let God use your situation that way.

DUANE:

I deal with it the same way a murderer or drug addict or any other former prisoner deals with the stigma of their criminal history. America loves to hate someone. Wait a few years and they will get tired of your crime and start in on someone else. Anyone remember the war on drugs and how that has turned out? Soon they will run out of other people to persecute and have only themselves left. I do know that if you harbor resentment towards these people you must resolve this issue and forgive when necessary, ask for forgiveness when necessary and keep your focus on Christ, not the world.

Regarding dealing with self-condemnation, I can't stop these attacks of the evil one from occurring. It is a constant battle. I rebuke these thoughts in the Name of Jesus and send them, and the evil source of these thoughts, back to the abyss where they came from. Jesus Christ came not to condemn the world, but to save it. Anything else is not of

His will for you, and you must simply rebuke it and keep your focus on the love that God has for you and His will for you to have a purpose-driven and prosperous life. Living in the past will not help you, it will destroy you. These thoughts are the work of the evil one and not of Christ Jesus.

I have come to believe that there is much you can do to help yourself. Yes, it is true that the Lord Jesus Christ can, and has healed my body, mind, and spirit in many ways at many times. But, there is much that I can do to help myself. I go to therapy once per week, as do all sex offenders. I have been through the sex offender treatment program. I have been blessed to have been exposed to self-help courses and programs while incarcerated.

These people, even though they work for the State and fall into that "them" category that I learned while in prison, have shown time and again that they are primarily concerned with my well-being. Yes, they must report any criminal activity I reveal to them to the authorities, but so do free-world counselors (I see one of them as well). They have told me how to talk about these issues to others that do not trigger this requirement yet still allow us to get it out into the open and work through the underlying issues. I encourage you to find a way to build a trusting relationship with these people or, if you cannot at this time do this, to find someone you can trust to talk about these things. Whatever the circumstances are that led to my situation, I need to get these issues resolved, and the old me is not able to do this without some help from a professional. I talk about these things to my Church family, but they are not always able to help me work through the issues that have caused me to act out in the way I did, and if I don't get these issues resolved, I risk reoffending. That is not part of the plan today.

I am not overwhelmed by my past because I turn it all over to God. Let the past be the past, not the present or the future. I only have to carry the burdens that I pick up. I cannot forget my past, and I don't want to forget, really, the wrongs I have committed. It has made me who I am today. I would not have the faith and knowledge of God's Love and Mercy as fully as I do if I had made other choices in my life, and while I regret the harm I have caused to my victims, my family, and myself, I embrace the healing I have been fortunate to receive from God and those people He has put in my life to bring me to where I am today. Sure, I would rather have come to this knowledge by another route, but it is what it is. I can bear any burden of my own creation and any other burden of this world with the strength that God provides, and if I follow His prompting I will live according to His will for me. In AA they said to let go and let God, and it is true. I can't change the route I took to get here, but I can choose where I go from here.

RUSSELL:

Yes, it can be hard! Even as a follower of Jesus, you have to really believe that you are a new creature in Christ and that He has forgiven your past.

You must forgive yourself. Put the past in the past and do not let the world or the enemy torment you over it. If you start feeling your past is the cause of job rejection or social out-casting, realize quickly that it is the enemy coming to roost and trying to take up residence in your soul and spirit man. Don't let him in and don't let him win! You have to cast out his attacks by taking your thoughts captive to the obedience of Christ. You are accepted by Jesus! Stand firm and continue walking in the Lord.

Whenever I start to feel the least bit overwhelmed, I just stop what I'm doing and let God take control. I must realize who I am in Him and know for certain He can lead me out of any situation.

The hardest thing I have to deal with is as a condition of parole is that I am required to attend therapy weekly. Every Saturday morning, I go to therapy and have to deal with going back to the crime that put me in prison. So having to deal with your past there can be one of the hardest things to do. I know I must stay strong in Christ because He helps me get through this and every trial. One thing that helps me is to continue to be grateful that He has allowed me to be back in the free world!

My family has abandoned me because of my charges and the way I lived before prison. Is there any real hope that God can and will restore broken relationships?

STEPHEN:

As my longer testimony disclosed earlier in this book, by the time I got to prison I had pushed away or offended every family member and close friend I ever had. My family hadn't heard from me in at least three years, and my former "friends" didn't want to ever hear from me again. On top of that, because of my crime and prison sentence, I didn't want to reach out to any of them either. I was too ashamed, guilt-ridden and embarrassed.

In my despair and emptiness, I turned to God and my Gideon New Testament even though I thought my life was over and that nothing would ever get better. As I began to understand His love and forgiveness for me, a small glimmer of hope began to creep in. I felt led to finally get past my pride and shame and write a letter to my family members to ask them to forgive me. I did not make it a long, detailed letter-only I ½ pages- but I told them I was sorry for the way I had treated them and asked them to forgive me. I also admitted where I was and why I was there. All this was very humbling, but a burden began to be lifted as I put it in the mail.

My two brothers wrote back quickly saying they were not holding anything against me. They said they were sorry to learn where I was and why I was there but they both asked what they could do to help me. Another weight was lifted off of my soul. They have never stopped loving me and offering their assistance. It took my younger sister a while after I got out of prison for her to see that God had really changed me but now we have a closer relationship than ever before. Even my son forgave me, and God is continuing to restore that long broken relationship.

When we really give our hearts to Jesus, the Holy Spirit begins His work in us to transform us into the people God intends and begins to unfold His perfect plan for us day by day. We must humble ourselves before God and others, and truly turn from our old way of life in repentance. God really does want to work in and through us to restore our families to us. But it is all in His timing and does not happen overnight. Many times, they have to see us in the free world continuing to be committed to Christ before they will begin to open up their hearts to us again. We must be patient, trust God, and keep serving Him faithfully even before we see the beginning of restoration. That's where faith comes in.

God has given me so many friends who also love Jesus. None of us are perfect, but we are forgiving, understanding and encouraging to one another. I am continually amazed at how Good and Gracious God is in restoring family and friends, and bringing other Christians into my life. Believe me, He wants to do the same for you. Do your part. He will do His. Keep praying. Keep believing.

BRANDON:

A lot of us have to deal with this regardless of our charges. I was not abandoned by my family, but what bothered me the most was abandoning my children for a combined seventeen years by being in prison. I prayed that God would mend my relationship with my five children and He has done that very thing! It amazes me that it's like I never went anywhere. It's only by God's grace. So, I know by my own experience God's ability to reconcile relationships.

I know of a man whose family completely cut him off due to his lifestyle before prison. He did over seventeen years as a result of his drug addiction. He gave his life to Christ and was eventually released. Once his mother and family saw the genuine change God had made in his life, the doors and lines of communication were open between him and his family. Their relationships were not only restored but strengthened (Mark 5:1-20).

DUANE:

There is always hope. My father always told me this while I was in prison when I told him that I would never be coming home. He remained true to this belief even when I began to get eleven years of set-offs. And I have just recently been reconciled with my son, whom I have not seen or heard from pretty much his entire life. I have spoken with my grandchildren, and other family who abandoned me while I was in prison. I can only say that I think they were just overwhelmed with grief and that was how they handled it. I am aware that some may have committed crimes against their family members which may have aggravated their grief, but there is always hope. I can only ask for God's forgiveness, make amends to and ask for forgiveness from my family, and pray that someday healing will come.

RUSSELL:

Yes, God can do anything! Restoring broken relationships is a process so you have to have faith and patience. Remember that you may have caused extreme hurt and pain because you were being selfish, not caring about all the others who may have been affected, especially among your family and friends. In my case, even in the first years of incarceration I was only thinking of myself.

God has also miraculously restored relationships in my life. It took years, but my family forgave me and we now enjoy spending time together.

As soon as I was released I was able to visit my mother who had dementia. My sister Cindy said, "Mom, look who is here!" She did not recognize me at first, then another God-miracle happened. It seemed as if God renewed her mind and we were able to have a two-hour lucid conversation.

When I was released, I had not seen my son, Chase, since 2009, when he came to visit me when I was on Smith Unit. We had a two-hour visit there. It was a contact visit, so we hugged and had a good talk.

Chase is now 34, and he came to see me at Kingdom Towers about three months after I arrived. We had a good visit. I am praying now that our relationship will deepen between us to the point that one day we will serve God together. Recently, he started helping me on some of the cleaning jobs I have!

God is Good all the time!

What advice would you give as to how to live as a truly committed Christian while still in prison?

STEPHEN:

Whether in prison or not, your heart must first be truly committed to God having come to faith in Christ Jesus through true repentance. True repentance doesn't just mean being sorry for your sins and confessing them to God, but turning away from them with the determination to never intentionally walk in that direction again. It is a heart set on wanting to please God instead of self and desiring to be obedient to God and His principles. It is a heart that repents immediately if you miss the mark, gets up quickly if you fall, and is determined to keep headed the right direction towards God instead of going back to your old way of life.

We all know how "close" prison really is in that everyone seems to know everything all the time! Living a life for Christ Jesus will definitely get you noticed in prison, but hopefully for the right reasons. We all know people are watching someone who is trying to follow God. Hypocrites talk a good game but they live differently. Those around you are inwardly wanting your transformation to be real because it gives them hope that God might do for them what He is doing in and through your life.

Establish a daily routine that gives God and His Word priority in your life. Daily prayer, Bible study, devotional readings and Bible Correspondence Courses are all positive ways to do your time rather than letting your time do you. Watch for people you can pray for or encourage. Go to as many Christian Chapel services or classes as you are allowed. If you have a radio, listen to Christian talk radio to learn from many good Christian teachers and preachers regularly. When you establish these productive habits and patterns you will find that your time goes much quicker.

When those times come when you say or do something that does not honor God, be sure to openly repent, ask forgiveness and do your best not to keep misrepresenting Jesus. Being sure to humble yourself, admitting you were wrong, and being willing to try to make it right, are all actions and attitudes that display a very powerful witness for Christ.

Do not be ashamed to read your Bible openly or to go to Chapel services with a smile on your face and a Bible in your hand. Look for opportunities to help or encourage others, especially those who are treated poorly or ignored by other prisoners.

If you have money in your account and it is not against your facility regulations, quietly give someone a surprise blessing on commissary day, especially those who rarely, if ever, make store. I remember a man who would often bring me a couple of peppermint candies during the first year I was incarcerated without any money on my books. It was a small act of kindness but it was always a treat for me. Sometimes I would find a Ramen Noodle Soup on my bunk, or someone would give me a honey bun. Done with a pure heart and no ulterior motive, these acts of blessing speak volumes about our love for Christ Jesus.

Pay attention to the way you talk, and do not participate in meaningless or destructive discussions. Don't participate in gossip or slander. You do not want to give the devil any glory by often discussing or re-living your past. If you have a problem with someone, go to them privately to try to resolve it, don't bad-mouth them to others.

Something else that causes others to question our Christian commitment is if we are participating in selling or receiving anything that is not rightfully ours. As a Christian you will not be selling or receiving stolen goods when you get back into the free world, so we should not be doing it inside. The same goes with drugs, tobacco or anything else that is often so prevalent in prison. The habits you are establishing now–whether good or bad–will carry on out into the free world.

We should also not be disrespecting the correctional officers, rank or staff; or otherwise talking bad about them behind their back. Pray for them regularly. They are people just like you, with their own set of problems and challenges, and God loves them too. Unbelievers, whether prisoners or correctional officers, are wanting to see that God is real to you. Sometimes you are the only "Jesus" they will ever see!

These are only a few suggestions, and I know you can think of others. You have a great opportunity to be the light in a dark place. Live your life each day in a way that honors God and well represents Jesus. Moment to moment, choose to be led by the Holy Spirit rather than being led by the world, the flesh and the devil. Be "all in" for Jesus every day.

BRANDON:

My advice to anyone who is truly committed to Christ, and who desires to live their lives sold out for Christ while in prison, would be not to live a life of compromise in any area. Do not allow prison culture to shape your Christianity.

John the Baptist stood out because he was different than the rest. He wore camel's hair garments with a leather belt and ate wild honey and locusts (Matthew 3:4-6). Similarly, we as children of God have to walk in a way that's worthy of the Lord among those who are in darkness. Be an example. Allow God to use you to be a light to others.

All this flows from a relationship with God. Jesus said, "If you love me keep my commandments", and "Love your neighbor as yourself." These things were very hard to do at times; I had to have the power of the Holy Spirit and the love of God residing in me. Relationship, relationship, relationship is my advice.

DUANE:

"Truly committed" is a judgement that I am not going to comment on. It has been my experience that people who use phrases like that have their own agenda tied into it. I look to the Lord for my salvation and healing. If I follow the prompting of the Holy Spirit in my life choices I will come to know the will of God for my life. Then I am a "committed" Christian. There are entirely too many people telling me how I should do this or that. Lean not on your own understanding, but seek His will for you and He will make of you a truly committed Christian.

Lastly, pray. Pray all the time. Talk to God just like you were talking to yourself. You don't need to kneel or pray in a loud voice. Just talk to him as if you were talking to yourself. Talk to Him about everything, especially the things that you are struggling with. He only wants what is good for you, the evil one wants what is going to hurt you. You can tell the difference between what God wants for you and what the evil one wants for you in the Word of God, His Bible. If what you are receiving is supported by the Word, then it is from God. The evil one can quote scripture, but what he prompts you to do is not going to be supported by scripture.

RUSSELL:

Be all in for God! If you give your life to Christ while in prison, you can be sure you will be under the microscope from non-Christians especially. They want you to fall in a big way so do not give them the satisfaction.

So my advice to you if you truly want to serve God, then serve God with all your heart. Always smile and be respectful to others. It's no cakewalk but by having a loving, giving heart you are doing things God wants. I recommend getting involved in Bible study groups and prayer groups, etc.

But always remember, if and when you fall or mess up, quickly repent, ask God's forgiveness, get up and keep walking on your journey to God. Your strength in Christ will be challenged, but just remember what the disciples went through and the problems they faced.

Don't ever give up, God will see you through!

Will I be able to go to Church while on parole? Will Churches accept someone who is an ex-convict, a former felon, or on the sex offender registry? Will I be able to volunteer in a Church like teaching classes, ushering, etc?

STEPHEN:

As far as I know, most parole officers will allow you to go to Church while you are on parole even if you are on a monitor, but this may vary somewhat by city and State.

Regarding which Churches will accept and welcome you, I am certain this varies among denominations, Pastors and individual congregations. I always recommend looking for a non-denominational, Spirit-filled Church that preaches Jesus Christ and the full Gospel.

I was recommended a particular one in Levelland, TX, to visit. After I had attended four or five weeks, and I thought it was one I was interested in possibly joining, I met with one of the Pastors to share my testimony and my charges. They appreciated my honesty and forthrightness and said I would be welcome to attend.

I joined and attended faithfully for about two years until another member who apparently knew I was a registered sex offender raised a concern that they thought I was regularly going to the children's area to pick up the granddaughter of a female friend. It was clear to me they were confusing me with another good friend of mine who was also attending regularly who was actually a very close friend of our mutual female friend. He regularly picked up the granddaughter, not me.

The associate Pastor asked to meet with three of us who they knew were former sex offenders and asked us to be very sensitive to all appearances. It was a reasonable request, and was generally done in a loving way. We all agreed, but it was clear to me that they had the most concern about me. I was not allowed to know or speak to my accuser, and I ultimately decided it was best if I looked for another church.

I found a great one in Lubbock, thirty miles away. After attending a few times, like before, I informed the Pastor before I decided to become a member of the Church. He welcomed me as a new man in Christ; and, and I never had one issue concerning my past as a felon and former sex offender. I was made to feel welcome and loved in every respect.

About two years later, after a member of our prison ministry started a new church, I left the previous Church on good terms. I explained to my former Pastor that I felt I needed to support our team member in his efforts to begin a new Word and Spirit, non-denominational Church. Since about 2013 when I left the first church, I have always been an active, supportive member of a good church and have never been made to feel unwelcome or shunned in any way because of my past. In fact, several churches provide financial support to our prison ministry, and many former offenders attend and are welcomed by these churches.

I believe God wants us to find a loving body of believers where our past is not held against us, and where we could volunteer to serve. My advice is to ask around after you arrive at your parole address, listen to the Spirit's leading, visit a few churches, and trust God to show you where He wants you. Be humble, be grateful, and extend to others the grace and love you want extended to you.

BRANDON:

From my own personal experience, I was released on a monitor on Thursday and was at my first church service that first Sunday! A year and a half later, I am still on an ankle monitor and parole but have never had any issues with the parole office, my parole officers, nor with registration about attending church.

I attended a Christian Conference in Lubbock and visited several churches before I found the church to which I felt God was calling me. Out of all the churches I visited, including the church I joined in the Fall, 2019, I have never had any negative encounters or attacks on me due to my past. I am not saying its not going to happen or couldn't happen, only for me I have not experienced it.

On the contrary, God has opened doors of opportunity for me to do various things in different ministries. This includes speaking, teaching classes, facilitating Bible studies, playing the drums and many other things. I believe the enemy tries to put a spirit of fear of not being accepted by the Body of Christ to isolate and mislead us. But more importantly we should always remember even Jesus Christ wasn't accepted (John 1:11). He never looked for or needed validation from men, only God (John 2:23-25).

DUANE:

I am attending two churches while on parole. My parole officers (I have two of them assigned to my case) are very supportive of my attendance at church and have not objected to my attending. I have no idea whether or not they contacted the church, but I have not heard anything about it if they have.

It is a simple thing for someone to find out if I am on the registry. I assume that if the churches I attend did do a background check on me that they did not care about my sexual convictions.

Whether or not to volunteer is a personal decision. I imagine that the church leaders will determine at the time of a request if what you wish to bring to the body of Christ is appropriate. I am involved in a Bible study at one of my churches before the regular service that is led by a former inmate. It has been a very rewarding study.

RUSSELL:

Yes, you will be able to attend church. I have not been rejected by any of the churches I have attended. The longer you attend and participate in as many activities as you feel called to, I believe you will eventually be allowed even more participation and privileges.

I began attending church upon arrival at Kingdom Towers in August, 2019. The following February, my friend Don Enger baptized me at Trinity Church in Lubbock. I still attend that church.

Don Enger started encouraging me to give my testimony at various places, and he set up appointments for me. So far, I have given my testimony at many places, including the Gideons, various churches, prime-timers at Trinity Church Lubbock, with other opportunities coming up soon. I have been warmly received by everyone, and thank God for His care for me in honoring Him through my testimony.

I also thank God that I facilitate two classes at Kingdom Towers, including a Bible class, and a Celebrate Recovery class.

Can an ex-convict, former felon, or former sex offender be licensed as a minister? Can they pastor a church? What should I be doing to prepare myself while I am incarcerated?

STEPHEN:

As far as I know, there is no regulation that would prevent a former felon or sex offender from being licensed and/or ordained; nor, do I know of any rule that would automatically disqualify them from pastoring a Church. The most important thing is to be sure God is calling you to this because it is a very serious and important, life-long commitment to God and His Kingdom.

Because a person's past would be subject to significant scrutiny, I advise anyone interested in being licensed or ordained to wait to pursue particular details and procedures of doing that until they are released. Upon release, I believe it is very important to first find a Church or ministry in which to serve. Ask the Pastor or ministry leader about the process of being licensed or ordained under them;

and, whether they would be willing to let you sit up under their mentorship and authority until they can help you determine when and how to pursue God's call.

Although there are some organizations that will consider licensing or ordaining you while you are incarcerated, I believe it is much better and more meaningful to wait to pursue this after your release.

As soon as I was released I contacted Don Castleberry, Chairman and Founder, of Freedom in Jesus Ministries, Inc. who had already agreed to mentor me and be an accountability partner for me. I began to serve as a volunteer in the ministry and met with Don for an hour or more, five days a week, for about four months. These were great sessions where "iron sharpened iron". After a year of serving under him, I asked to be ordained and licensed as I felt certain God had a call on my life to a deeper commitment in the Kingdom of God. He ordained and licensed me into the Gospel Ministry in February, 2012, after I had been with him for over a year. In 2015, I became the full-time Executive Director of the ministry and, in 2020, was made President.

While you are incarcerated, I encourage you to pursue as much Biblical knowledge as possible. If there is a correspondence course of study leading to one or more degrees in Theology or Biblical Studies, I recommend you complete them with sincerity and diligence. Although I did not pursue a degree in Theology, I completed every Bible Correspondence course I could find while I was incarcerated, was actively involved in Chaplaincy classes and services several times a week; studied my Bible daily for significant periods of time; and led Bible study/ prayer groups in my housing area daily.

BRANDON:

The first question is easy to answer for me because I received my ministry license even though I was a sex offender. There were no unusual hoops I had to jump through, nor were there restrictions that hindered me from going through the normal process of ordination.

I personally know two men who are senior pastors over their churches. Both of them had cases involving a minor. Certainly they use wisdom in letting their congregations know of their past, as well as sitting down with new members personally to inform them of their past (Hebrews 5:1-4). If God has called and sent you there is nothing anyone can do to stop God's purpose and plan for your life. Whatever God has called you to do, do it!

While I was incarcerated after giving my life to Christ I sought God with all my heart through many hours of studying and prayer. I encourage anyone who is serious about living their lives for Christ to do the same, especially if you know God has called you into leadership.

DUANE:

Any vocation that you would like to pursue will have regulations or policies whether or not you are able to do this because of your criminal history. Talk to your church leaders about this and they will advise you as to whether or not you can do this and how to go about preparing yourself. I know many former prisoners who have earned degrees, both inside and outside of prison, who have given sermons and talks to groups of people. Some of them have even started their own ministry.

RUSSELL:

I defer to the previous answers as I have no direct knowledge of this.

How often do you have to register as a sex offender, or update the registry, after you are released? Have you looked in the legal process for de-registering? If you are registered, but off parole, does life return to pretty much normal? How long does a person stay on the sex offender registry?

STEPHEN:

Upon my release from prison in late 2010, I had to immediately update the sex offender registry from 2007 when I was first registered. I did this in the county where I was released in Nashville as I discussed in an earlier question. If I had been on parole, I think I would have also had to immediately meet with a parole officer.

As soon as I arrived in Levelland, TX, I was told I have to personally report to the Police Department officer in charge of registered sex offenders in my city, Levelland, TX, once a year around my birth date. I was also required to annually renew my driver's license and give them a copy. Any time I wanted to move, I had to get their permission in advance for the new address. If I changed vehicles, I was required to immediately provide the license number and other details about the vehicle. If I changed jobs, I would be required to immediately report it so they could update their records.

The city where I live, Levelland, TX, is a small city of about 12,500 people. Levelland is 30 miles west of Lubbock, TX. Every city or county has their own unique policies and procedures as to when and how rigorously they will enforce the many details in the state sex offender registry laws. In my own experience and according to my very basic understanding, the person to whom you are reporting will explain the major parts of the law and have you sign a summary they will give you.

I have never been required to take an annual lie detector test, which I assume is because I wasn't on parole. However, it may be that Levelland does not have the policy to require one. I know former sex offenders who are still on parole that do in fact have to submit to a polygraph annually.

Also, I was not required to attend any kind of weekly classes for former sex offenders after my release; again, I assume that was because I was not on parole. However, for the brief time in the fall of 2007 when I was first on probation and on the registry in Tennessee, there were requirements for periodic meetings with a counselor, and I think I was subject to the requirement for an annual polygraph, although I was locked up before I actually had to take one.

I have not looked into the process and cost of de-registering although I was contacted by a law firm advertising their services in this regard. Since the nature of my case was such that I could come off the registry after ten years with a clean record, I did not think it was worth my time and money to pursue de-registering. However, if I was scheduled to stay on the registry for life, I would have definitely looked into it. I heard it cost at least $5,000 but I am sure each law firm is different, and that their rates would vary depending on each person's unique circumstances and their time required to represent them.

Having not been on parole, I guess you could say my life is as normal as it could get while still being subject to all the requirements I mentioned above. I certainly believe God's Hand of favor has been on me since my release in late 2010, so I know that I have not been subject to some of the requirements that I hear others face in cities and counties that are larger and more aggressive in strictly enforcing the registration laws.

Regarding how long a person is on the sex offender registry, I believe it may vary somewhat by state. For what might be classified as "less serious" offenses you may be able to come off the registry after ten years. My crime was "solicitation of a minor" and, in March, 2021, I was told I have been released from the requirements and removed from the Sex Offender Registry. I don't know what other crimes might fall into this category and you might not be able to find out for sure until you are released. If my crime hadn't fallen in this category, I think I would have been required to register for life. I do not think it has anything to do with when you are released from parole.

BRANDON:

I defer to Stephen's answer above. I have not looked in to the legal process for de-registering. From my understanding each case and charge carries its own length of registration.

DUANE:

I am required to register every year on my birthday. I have to update my information as required: if I change my appearance, move, go to school, etc. This was all explained to me when I registered, and each case has different criteria, but all registered sex offenders have things they must do while on parole. Once you are off paper things change, but I am not conversant about what these are, as I will never be off paper. The Sexual Offender Registration Officers were very different than I had imagined they would be. They were not overbearing or threatening. They did let me know that I did not want them investigating me, but if I kept my nose clean, I would be okay. I have not had any problem from them or the police here in Lubbock.

RUSSELL:

I have to report to the registration officer every three months. I believe it varies based on the seriousness of your charges; some people only report every twelve months. I have not looked into deregistration. I was told I have to register for ten more years after I finish parole.

As to life returning to normal, my opinion is it primarily depends on you. Sure, it's hard to adjust when you get out, but if you have a strong mind/will and are living for the Lord Jesus, things will fall into place. Your past does not define you; forgive yourself and move forward.

Do some cities, counties and states treat former sex offenders less harshly? Is the public notified of sex offenders in their area?

STEPHEN:

I am only familiar with the small city in Texas where I live but I have heard numerous times that every city, county or State is different. It is probably very difficult to know many details until you get settled into your parole address destination. My advice is to go "all in" with Jesus now, and trust God to walk through all this with you as it comes up. I would not put confidence in what man says about conditions in the "free world" for former sex offenders, knowing that it is God Who has the final say. Much of what you hear are unfounded rumors anyway. Your eternal destination is most important, so be sure you have an intimacy of personal relationship with Jesus every day.

Some cities and counties notify the public in various ways regarding former sex offenders living in the area, but this was not the case in Levelland, or Hockley County, TX, where I live. I have been told that sometimes post cards are mailed out to the immediate vicinity when a new sex offender moves into the area. I also know that sometimes their picture may be posted briefly on television. None of this happened to me.

However, with the age of the internet, a person can look up the sex offender registry for their state and locality. With GPS now, I understand that a person can be shown where former sex offenders live in their immediate vicinity or neighborhood block.

In my case, I have only had one neighbor about 1 ½ blocks away confront me with knowledge that I was on the sex offender registry. It wasn't a pleasant conversation but there was no physical violence. Clearly, he had a bias against my crime and primarily wanted me to know not to come around his house or children. Certainly, I had no intention of doing so, but I changed my route for my daily walk to avoid his house to lessen the chances of confrontation or false accusation.

BRANDON:

I have heard of some states having less harsh requirements for sex offenders. All sex offenders are required to register and the information is available to the public.

Personally, I have never had any situation where I have been confronted or harassed because of my past or my charge. While incarcerated I heard so many horror stories that caused me to fear that my life was over, but in reality, things have not been anywhere close to what I was made to believe. God has opened up doors for me that others who have never been in any trouble at all couldn't go through.

As I have done my best to keep every area of my life God-centered, He has made my transition back into society unbelievably smooth.

DUANE:

I have no direct knowledge of how other states treat sex offenders. I do know that each county and large city in Texas has different rules, so it seems reasonable to assume that the states treat sex offenders differently. I would not even say that I have been treated harshly. My parole officers are, within the limitations of their authority, very supportive and understanding. The Sexual Offender Registration Officers have not sought me out for harassment or anything. All in all, while it has not been a paradise, it has not been a hell either.

RUSSELL:

Although I have no knowledge of how it is in other States I believe Texas may be one of the harsher States on sex offenders. When your stipulations are laid on you, you have to do your best to meet the requirements. You cannot live in fear for we know "God does not give us a spirit of fear, rather of power, love and a sound mind" (2 Timothy 1:7).

For those offenders whose charges involved a minor (someone under 18), or involved child pornography charges, what special restrictions might there be compared to someone whose charges involved only adults? Do I need a parole address that is not near to schools, etc.? Can I attend church? Am I allowed to go to school functions and ball games with my kids? Can I talk to a youth group or school group with a chaperone, or do I need to be off parole? Can I have more children with my spouse after my release?

STEPHEN:

As I stated earlier, my crime was solicitation of a minor, so some of the above questions I am able to address. However, I did not have minor children when I was released, and I have not gotten married, so specific questions involving children in the family are some with which I have no personal experience. Also, since I was not on parole, I am not fully versed in what they may or may not require or allow.

For offenders whose crime involved a minor or child pornography, as opposed to those with crimes involving only adults, there are a number of additional restrictions. For example, generally you cannot live within 1,000 feet (a little less than a quarter of a mile) of a school, park or a children's day care business. My understanding is that it is okay for you to live within a 1,000 feet of a church if it does not have a children's day care operation on weekdays. Again, my understanding is that there are not usually such restrictions affecting where a person lives whose crimes involved an adult.

Some wonder why a transition facility that accepts sex offenders involving adults cannot accept offenders with crimes involving minors. Usually, it is only because the transition facility is too close to a school, park or day care. Although our ministry is closely associated with them, this is the only reason why Kingdom Towers in Lubbock, TX, cannot accept former sex offenders involving a minor whereas they can accept those involving an adult.

Another common restriction for offenders whose crime involved a minor is not to go to public parks, or be around schools while they are in session even though the person may not live close to them. Depending upon the registry requirements and enforcement in your area, the location of your place of employment may have also have to take into account the proximity to schools, parks and day care facilities.

The parole office may have some different requirements for offenders whose crimes involved minors. For example, the parole officer most likely has to give prior approval before attending church, or prior to being involved in any way with youth groups, but I am not aware of any general prohibition forever restricting this involvement. I believe most parole officers have been given guidance to allow parolees to go to church once a week, but this might not be the case especially in the first few weeks. Also, they may not let you go to church more than once a week in the early stages of parole supervision.

One thing I think we all need to be aware of after our release is to try to intentionally avoid every situation where there could be any question of our intent or motives. I want to do everything I can not to put myself in a position where false accusations could be made, especially involving minors. I am not concerned from a "temptation" standpoint as to who I used to be, rather it is about avoiding even an unfounded suspicion of anything.

For example, at church I do not go anywhere near the children's or youth areas. I am careful not to engage children much even in public unless their parents are present with them. Although I am an ordained and licensed minister, I would not ever work with youth groups or children as a volunteer in the church of which I am a member. The Bible says we should avoid even the appearance of evil. Personally, for myself, these same principles would apply if I attended a ball game or school function.

Although I do not know this for certain, I would find it difficult to believe that the state could prevent a person from having other children with their spouse. However, there may be a period of time after release that visits with your children would have to be supervised if you could not get approved to parole to their residence.

BRANDON:

My charge did not involve a minor, so I cannot answer these questions specifically. However, I still walk in wisdom, making sure I do not put myself in a position that could present a risk of a false accusation and thereby jeopardize my freedom. My life is normal, good and fulfilling!

All the concerns, worries and fears that tried to attach themselves to me while incarcerated God has proven to be a lie from the enemy. I wasted a lot of mental and emotional energy listening to and believing negative opinions and falsehoods whether they came from inmates, officers or society.

DUANE:

My charges did not involve a minor.

RUSSELL:

My charges did not involve a minor.

Were you concerned other prisoners would find out about your charges? Were you ever attacked in prison because of being a sex offender? Were you rejected by other prisoners because of your charges? Should I lie about my charges to protect myself?

STEPHEN:

Although it should not be this way, others sometimes judge sex offenders in prison more critically than anyone else. I am not sure why this is generally true since almost everyone in prison is guilty of their own crimes. What's the old saying, "People who live in glass houses shouldn't throw stones?"

Before I was saved in prison, I never knew Jesus Himself said, "Let the one who is without sin throw the first stone." This was when a group of "religious" people brought an adulterous woman to Jesus asking if they should stone her according to the law of Moses. See John 8:1-11.

Certainly, I was anxious that my charge would become known and that I might be the subject of assault, discrimination or shame. I was never physically assaulted for that reason, only for having a really smart mouth when I first got to county jail! I was getting involved in a discussion that didn't really involve me. I learned some lessons from that but it had nothing to do with my charges.

After I was saved in prison, and serving the Lord the best I could, I was publically "outed" once by a prison counselor/corrections officer who was not a believer and thought, I guess, that I was a fake Christian. In front of a number of people she angrily yelled at me and accused me of being a "child molester". I was angry and embarrassed. It certainly occurred to me that she may have put me in danger so I was initially anxious about that aspect too.

After seeking the Lord, and praying with a few guys in the Bible study group I led nightly, I was encouraged that I must trust God for His protection, grace and favor. That's what I did. Nothing worse developed from that situation because, I believe, of God's mercy and protection.

I never directly lied about my charges. Since the crime for which I was arrested was heavily influenced by drugs and alcohol, if someone asked me why I was locked up, I generally just said it was "drug-related" and changed the subject, or walked away. Although I have been much more open and transparent about my charges since my release, I did not speak about it in prison. While I was incarcerated, I prayed regularly for wisdom from God as to how to handle situations if they ever arose. I believe He honored my prayers.

Certainly, there have been times both inside and outside of prison where I have been rejected because of my past. Jesus was rejected too. The Bible says He took on all of my rejection so that I could receive

His acceptance with the Father. I remind myself that I would always rather please God rather than man. I know I am accepted by the Father because of the Son, Jesus!

BRANDON:

At the beginning of my incarceration I was very much ashamed of my charge and fearful that others would find out, not out of fear of conflict or anything physical. It was more out of not wanting to be looked down upon.

I have never been attacked or confronted about my charge, even after God gave me the boldness and courage to share my story openly so He could use it as a tool to encourage others around me. I can't say I was rejected by others because of my charge but I am sure I was the topic of some rumors or haters but nothing other than that.

It never came to me in a negative way. Some people would ask me about it and I would share my story with them. I don't believe lying about it will help anyone in prison. Generally, there is no sure way to conceal that kind of information. Most people will respect the honest approach in the long run even if they don't like the truth. More importantly as soldiers of Christ, we stand on the truth even when consequences follow. Never lie, but use wisdom as well.

DUANE:

Sure, but running from my sexual misconduct is not productive to my rehabilitation and keeping secrets is a sure way in for the evil one to work on you. I did not go around telling people what I was in for, and it's none of their business, but if you develop a close relationship with someone you have to be honest with them.

I had some situations while in prison, but whether or not they were motivated because of a knowledge of my crimes I do not know.

Regarding rejection, yes, but those people who are in prison being judgmental towards others are not the people with whom I wished to continue to associate myself. I don't associate with them out here, either.

It is my personal opinion that you should never lie about your problems. It develops into a habit that will impede your rehabilitation and hinder you from resolving your issues. However, if you are afraid that you will be targeted because of your criminal history, you must do something to protect yourself. I would caution you that there are many ways an individual can find out your criminal history these days, even in prison.

RUSSELL:

Yes, I was concerned! However, I went into the system in the mid-1980's, and if you stood up for yourself no one cared why you were in prison. This might have been because sex offenders with minors and other people with high profile cases were kept in protective custody. Plus, back then you minded your own business and there was respect.

So, having said that, in 2015, my charges became known to the Aryan Brotherhood on the unit where I was assigned. I think because of my age, and the stature and respect I had gained as an "old-timer" they just let me know they wouldn't touch me, and some of them didn't even let it bother them.

In 2016, I was shipped to a unit where a female kitchen officer was raped and killed about three weeks after I got on the unit so it was really hard on all sex offenders for a while. But, by the grace of God, I was protected for the rest of my time there and never had any issues. Although I established some good relationships, in many respects I regret that I was not always totally honest with them. Certainly a person should pray for Godly wisdom for each situation knowing that God always honors honesty.

INFORMATION FOR FURTHER
STUDY AND APPLICATION

PRAYERS OF SUBMISSION

DAILY PRAYER OF SURRENDER AND SUBMISSION

Father God, I humbly surrender and submit myself fully to You and your leadership by Your Holy Spirit.

Lord, please forgive me for both my willful and my unintentional sins. Help me to freely and fully forgive others as You forgive me.

Father, I submit willingly and completely to your Hand as The Potter. Re-make me into the person You want me to be for the plan You have for me in Your perfect will. As You do, conform me to the image of Jesus by the sanctifying work of Your Holy Spirit.

Father, by Your grace help me to always be a grateful, humble heir of all Your promises; an obedient, faithful servant of all Your commands; a persistent, bold witness of Your salvation through Jesus; and, a loving, trusting child full of Your love. I surrender to Your Holy Spirit's leadership.

Let me be patient and persevering in prayer, ever watchful and responsive for opportunities to bless others as You have blessed me.

Empower me Father with Your grace, through the Spirit of Jesus in me, to diligently seek You and Your eternal Kingdom, so that I will not be distracted and overcome with the temptations and temporary pleasures of this alien world. In everything I think, say and do today, Father, let me continually glorify and honor You.

I love You, Jesus. I praise You and adore You for first loving me. Thank You for being made sin for me so that I am made righteous in You. Please love and bless others through me today as I seek to know and do Your perfect will for my life. I want to be led today by Your Holy Spirit in me.

In the power of the blood of Jesus, and the authority of His Name I pray. Amen.

PRAYER OF SUBMISSIVE OBEDIENCE IN A PARTICULAR AREA

Father, You are worthy of all praise, honor, and glory. I adore You. I worship You. I praise Your Holy Name.

Lord, You have been so patient with me, and I thank You. I also recognize Your still, small voice, speaking to me about an area of my life that needs resolution. You have been reminding me of my need to move ahead in this certain area, and I confess that I have not yet obeyed You. Please forgive me for my hesitation.

Today, I declare that I will take the step of faith You have spoken to me about. Lord, in regard to this step that I have been hesitant to take, I put away all my reluctance now, and I pledge to You that I will obey You.

And Lord, in those matters where I have been doing what You would prefer that I not do, I lay them aside, so that I can make room to do what You want me to do.

This is the way I choose to walk with you from now on. Laying aside my hesitancy and stubbornness, I step boldly, choosing You and Your purposes for my life. I declare that I will follow You in obedience.

Thank You, Lord! In Jesus' Name I pray. Amen.

Note: "The Prayer of Submissive Obedience in a Particular Area" was from a teaching by Derek Prince, www.derekprince.org.

BAPTISM IN THE HOLY SPIRIT– SCRIPTURAL BASIS AND AUTHORITY

JOHN THE BAPTIST TAUGHT ABOUT THE HOLY SPIRIT:

Matthew 3:11 "I baptize you with water for repentance. But after me will come one who is more powerful than I, whose sandals I am not fit to carry. He will baptize you with the Holy Spirit and with fire."

JESUS CHRIST HAD TO HAVE THE HOLY SPIRIT:

Matthew 3:16-17 As soon as Jesus was baptized, he went up out of the water. At that moment heaven was opened, and he saw the Spirit of God descending like a dove and lighting on him. And a voice from heaven said, "This is my Son, whom I love; with him I am well pleased."

JESUS NEEDED TO BE LED BY THE HOLY SPIRIT:

Matthew 4:1 Then Jesus was led by the Spirit into the desert to be tempted by the devil.

Luke 4:1 Jesus, full of the Holy Spirit, returned from the Jordan and was led by the Spirit in the desert...

JESUS WAS EMPOWERED BY THE HOLY SPIRIT:

Luke 4:14 Jesus returned to Galilee in the power of the Spirit, and news about him spread through the whole countryside.

Luke 4:18-19 "The Spirit of the Lord is on me, because he has anointed me to preach good news to the poor. He has sent me to proclaim freedom for the prisoners and recovery of sight for the blind, to release the oppressed, to proclaim the year of the Lord's favor."

Acts 10:38 ...how God anointed Jesus of Nazareth with the Holy Spirit and power, and how he went around doing good and healing all who were under the power of the devil, because God was with him.

YOU CAN HAVE THE HOLY SPIRIT AS A GIFT:

Luke 11:11-13 "Which of you fathers, if your son asks for a fish, will give him a snake instead? Or if he asks for an egg, will give him a scorpion? If you then, though you are evil, know how to give good gifts to your children, how much more will your Father in heaven give the Holy Spirit to those who ask him!"

John 7:37-39 On the last and greatest day of the Feast, Jesus stood and said in a loud voice, "If anyone is thirsty, let him come to me and drink. Whoever believes in me, as the Scripture has said, streams of living water will flow from within him." By this he meant the Spirit, whom those who believed in him were later to receive. Up to that time the Spirit had not been given, since Jesus had not yet been glorified.

Revelation 22:17 The Spirit and the bride say, "Come!" And let him who hears say, "Come!" Whoever is thirsty, let him come; and whoever wishes, let him take the free gift of the water of life.

John 14:16-17 "And I will ask the Father, and he will give you another Counselor to be with you forever— the Spirit of truth. The world cannot accept him, because it neither sees him nor knows him. But you know him, for he lives with you and will be in you."

Acts 1:4-5 On one occasion, while he was eating with them, he gave them this command: "Do not leave Jerusalem, but wait for the gift my Father promised, which you have heard me speak about. For John baptized with water, but in a few days you will be baptized with the Holy Spirit."

Acts 2:1-4 When the day of Pentecost came, they were all together in one place. Suddenly a sound like the blowing of a violent wind came from heaven and filled the whole house where they were sitting. They saw what seemed to be tongues of fire that separated and came to rest on each of them. All of them were filled with the Holy Spirit and began to speak in other tongues as the Spirit enabled them.

THE BAPTISM OF THE HOLY SPIRIT IS SEPARATE FROM WATER BAPTISM:

John 20:21-22 Again Jesus said, "Peace be with you! As the Father has sent me, I am sending you." And with that he breathed on them and said, "Receive the Holy Spirit."

Acts 8:14-17 When the apostles in Jerusalem heard that Samaria had accepted the word of God, they sent Peter and John to them. When they arrived, they prayed for them that they might receive the Holy Spirit, because the Holy Spirit had not yet come upon any of them; they had simply been baptized into the name of the Lord Jesus. Then Peter and John placed their hands on them, and they received the Holy Spirit.

Acts 19:1-6 While Apollos was at Corinth, Paul took the road through the interior and arrived at Ephesus. There he found some disciples and asked them, "Did you receive the Holy Spirit when you believed?" They answered, "No, we have not even heard that there is a Holy Spirit." So Paul asked, "Then what baptism did you receive?" "John's baptism," they replied. Paul said, "John's baptism was a baptism of repentance. He told the people to believe in the one coming after him, that is, in Jesus." On hearing this, they were baptized into the name of the Lord Jesus. When Paul placed his hands on them, the Holy Spirit came on them, and they spoke in tongues and prophesied.

THE HOLY SPIRIT

The Holy Spirit is the third person in the Trinity. He is fully God. He is eternal, omniscient, omnipresent, has a will, and can speak. He is alive. He is a person. He is not as visible in the Bible as the Son or Father because His ministry is to bear witness of them (John 15:26). However, as you begin to focus on Him, you will see how very important He is to us!

In the Old Testament the Hebrew word ruwach (pronounced roo'-akh) was used when talking about the Spirit. This word literally means WIND or BREATH. In the New Testament the Greek word pneuma (pronounced pnyoo'-mah) was used which means the BREATH or a BREEZE. We can literally think of the Holy Spirit as the "BREATH OF GOD."

Throughout the ages, many people have thought of the Holy Spirit as more of a "thing", or a "force", than a "Person." Nothing could be further from the truth. In fact, as we begin to know the Person of the Holy Spirit, we will want to have a closer relationship with Him just as we would the Father or Son.

The truth is that the Holy Spirit is a Person the same as the Father and Son are Persons within the Trinity.

By careful study of the following scriptures about the Person of God the Holy Spirit, you will be able to better understand His Presence and Power living in you:

HIS NAMES	HIS ATTRIBUTES	SYMBOLS OF	SINS AGAINST	POWER IN CHRIST'S LIFE
God Acts 5:3-4	Eternal Heb. 9:14	Dove Matt. 3:16	Blasphemy Matt. 12:31	Conceived of Matt. 1:18,20
Lord 2 Cor. 3:18	Omnipotent Luke 1:35	Wind Acts 2:1-4	Resist (Unbelief) Acts 7:51	Baptism Matt. 3:16
Spirit 1 Cor. 2:10	Omnipresent Psalm 139:7-10	Fire Acts 2:3	Insult Heb. 10:29	Led by Luke 4:1
Spirit of God 1 Cor. 3:16	Will 1 Cor. 12:11	Living Waters John 7:38-39 1 Cor. 12:13	Lied to Acts 5:3	Filled with Power Luke 4:14,18
Spirit of Truth John 15:26	Loves Rom. 15:30	•••••	Grieved Eph. 4:30	Witness of Jesus John 15:26
Eternal Spirit Heb. 9:14	Speaks Acts 8:29; 13:2	•••••	Quenched 1 Thess. 5:19	Raised Jesus Rom. 8:11
The Person of God the Holy Spirit				

Although the word Trinity is not mentioned in the Bible, we know God is three in one. There are three very distinct Persons that make up the Godhead. They are all equal in every way. The Holy Spirit is a Person the same as the Father and the Son are Persons within the Trinity. There are some who believe the Holy Spirit is merely a force. If this were true, then He could not speak (Acts 13:2); He could not be grieved (Eph. 4:30); and He would not have a will (1 Cor. 12:11).

It is important to understand the Holy Spirit is truly God because of the fact that if we are born again He lives in us. What we allow ourselves to become a part of we are inviting God to be part of. 1 Cor. 6:19.

FOUR IMPORTANT PRINCIPLES TO REMEMBER:

1. The Holy Spirit is God. Like the Father and the Son, He is a Person, not a "force", a "thing", or an "it".

2. We cannot focus on the Holy Spirit too much. Why? What is the Holy Spirit's mission? To reveal Jesus. What is Jesus' mission? To reveal the Father. What about the Father.....to send Jesus and the Holy Spirit so we can come to Him. Perfect Harmony. They never had a crisis management meeting in Heaven. They never tried to sit down and work things out. They never had a power struggle amongst themselves.

3. The Holy Spirit gives gifts for use in ministry and empowers effective ministry. 1 Cor. 12:7-11

4. The Holy Spirit gives us fruit which develops in us Christ-like character. Gal. 5:22-23

QUALITIES THAT A PERSON HAS.... (A "FORCE" OR "THING" DOES NOT):

1. The Holy Spirit has intellect. I Cor. 2:10

2. The Holy Spirit has knowledge. I Cor. 2:11

3. The Holy Spirit has emotions. Ephesians 4:30

4. The Holy Spirit has his own will and he makes decisions. Acts 16:6

5. The Holy Spirit loves. Romans 15:30

THINGS ONLY A PERSON WOULD DO (A "FORCE" OR "THING" DOES NOT):

1. He teaches you things about God and yourself. John 14:26

2. He tells the truth. John 15:26

3. He guides. John 16:13

4. He convinces. John 16:8

5. He prays for you. Romans 8:26-27

6. He commands. Acts 13:2

THE HOLY SPIRIT WAS ON THE SCENE LONG BEFORE THE DAY OF PENTECOST:

- He moved upon the face of the waters and was the active agent in creation. Jesus was the Word, the Holy Spirit moved. John 1:1,14; Genesis 1:2

- The Holy Spirit gave us the Word of God. 2 Peter 1:20-21

- The Holy Spirit regenerates our spirit when we accept Jesus Christ into our life. John 3:6

IN FACT, THE HOLY SPIRIT HAS ALWAYS WORKED HAND-IN-HAND WITH JESUS CHRIST:

- His birth. Matthew 1:20

- The life and ministry of Jesus. Luke 4:1; Luke 4:18

- His death and offering Himself as the perfect sacrifice. Hebrews 9:14

- The resurrection of Jesus – Actually all 3 members of the Godhead had a part in the resurrection! FATHER (Eph. 1:19-20); SON (John 10:18); HOLY SPIRIT (Romans 1:4).

- The main purpose of the Holy Spirit is to tell us about Jesus and Glorify Him. John 16:13-14

PENTECOST:

- Jesus said it was imperative that He go or the Spirit would not be sent. John 16:7

- Jesus felt it important enough for them to wait until the Spirit came to empower them. Acts 1:4-8

- Jesus' own mother needed the baptism of the Holy Spirit to be an effective witness. Acts 1:14

- On the day of Pentecost, the believers who were assembled in the Upper Room experienced a new Baptism, the one which John referred to. Acts 2:1-4

MINISTRY OF THE BAPTISM OF THE HOLY SPIRIT

Hebrews 6:17 **Malachi 3:6**	God's purpose is unchanging, confirmed and guaranteed.
Matthew 28:20	He is always with us through His Holy Spirit.
John 14:12 **Matthew 28:18**	The Holy Spirit enables us to do greater works than Jesus through the authority of Jesus given to us.
Hebrews 13:8	"Jesus Christ is same yesterday, today, and forever."

WHO IS THE HOLY SPIRIT?

Genesis 1:2,26	The Holy Spirit is the 3rd person of the Trinity.
1 Corinthians 12:11	He has a will.
Ephesians 4:30	He has feelings.
Luke 1:35	He conceived Jesus.

THE HOLY SPIRIT'S MINISTRY

John 14:15-18 **John 15:26-27** **John 16:13-15**	The Holy Spirit has been given to us that we may let Jesus work in and through us (our sole purpose in life is to carry the Holy Spirit in our body and let Him work through us that the Father might be glorified in the Son).
Romans 8:26-27	He makes intercession for us when we don't know how to pray.
John 14:16	He is our Helper and Teacher.
John 16:8	The Holy Spirit convicts. It is not our place to judge others; we are to let the Holy Spirit convict them.
Ephesians 4:30	He seals us for the day of redemption.
1 Corinthians 12:7-11	He distributes His manifestation gifts to us.
Hebrews 10:15	He witnesses to us (bears witness).
Romans 8:11	The Holy Spirit dwells in us and gives life to our mortal bodies
Acts 9:31	He comforts and encourages us.
Galatians 5:22-23	He bears fruit in us.
John 16:14	The Holy Spirit always glorifies Jesus.
1 Corinthians 12:13 **and Acts 1:5**	He baptizes.
Acts 1:8 and **Luke 24:49**	He endues power.

FIVE ACCOUNTS IN THE BOOK OF ACTS OF THE BAPTISM OF THE HOLY SPIRIT

Acts 2:4, Acts 8:14-25, Acts 9:17-20,
Acts 10:44-48, Acts 19:1-7

HOW TO RECEIVE THE BAPTISM OF THE HOLY SPIRIT

Jesus is the Baptizer of the Holy Spirit: Matthew 3:11,
Mark 1:8, Luke 3:16
Believe, Pray, Ask, Receive

MORE INFORMATION ON THE BAPTISM IN THE HOLY SPIRIT

SCRIPTURE REFERENCES

The Day of Pentecost	Acts 2
Spirit of power, love and a sound mind	2 Timothy 1:7
Sending another Counselor	John 14:15-20; John 16:7
Quenching the Spirit	1 Thessalonians 5:19-22
Receive the Holy Spirit	John 20:22
Joel's Prophecy	Joel 2:28-32
Test the Spirits	1 Thessalonians 5:21; 1 John 4:1
You will know them by their fruit	Matthew 7:15-20

SOME HOLY SPIRIT MANIFESTATIONS IN SCRIPTURE

- There is no comprehensive list... the Bible does not record all possible experiences (John 21:25).

- Falling under the influence of the Spirit (Revelation 1:17; Matthew 17:6; John 18:6; Acts 9:4-8; Ezekiel 1:28; 3:23, 43:3, 44:4; Daniel 8:17-18; Daniel 10:8-9).

- Drunk in the Spirit (Acts 2:15; Ephesians 5:18).

- Laughter and joy (Romans 14:17; Galatians 5:22; Psalm 126:2-3; Genesis 21:3,6; 1 Peter 1:8).

- Trembling and terror (Daniel 8:17-18, 10:7-11; Matthew 17:6; Matthew 28:4).

- Shaking (Exodus 19:16-18; Acts 4:31; Isaiah 6:4).

- Speechless (Daniel 10:15-19; Ezekiel 3:26; Luke 1:22).

- Weeping (2 Chronicles 34:27; Hosea 12:4; Matthew 26:75; Luke 19:41; 2 Corinthians 7:10; Revelation 5:4; Hebrews 5:7).

- Trances (Acts 10:10, 22:17; Numbers 24:3-4).

- Pockets of power (1 Samuel 19:19-24).

- Traveling by the Spirit (Acts 8:39-40; Ezekiel 3:14, 8:3, 11:24; 2 Corinthians 12:1-4, Revelation 4:1-2).

- Fire (Exodus 3:2, 24:17, 40:38; Leviticus 9:24; Luke 3:16; Acts 2:3; 1 Thessalonians 5:19; Hebrews 12:29).

CONFESSIONS FOR EVERY DAY

Loved One in Christ–Build your faith and claim God's promises for yourself by reading these confessions of God's Word aloud (thoughtfully and prayerfully – with conviction) every day. Keep doing it until they are your thoughts so that you can use the Word against Satan to "take every thought captive" when he attacks your mind! To "confess" is to say the same thing as God, so that as the Word transforms your mind, His thoughts become your thoughts! Confess these daily at least once – early morning is best so you are "armed and dangerous" when Satan attacks during the day! Before bedtime is good too so you are protected as you rest.

- I am not just an ordinary man/woman. I'm a child of the living God.

- I am not just a person; I'm an heir of God, and a joint heir with Jesus Christ. I'm not "just an old sinner", I am a new creation in Jesus, my Lord. I'm part of a chosen generation, a Royal Priesthood, a Holy Nation. I'm one of God's people. I am His. I am a living witness of His grace, mercy and love!

- I have been crucified with Christ and I no longer live, but Christ lives in me! The life I live in the body, I live by the faith of the Son of God, who loved me, and gave Himself for me. When the devil tries to resurrect the "old man", I will rebuke him and remind him sternly that I am aware of his tricks, lures, lies and deception. The "old man" is dead. My "new man" knows all old things are passed away–all things have become new!

- I'm not under guilt or condemnation. I refuse discouragement, for it is not of God. God is the God of all encouragement. There is therefore now no condemnation for those in Christ Jesus. Satan is a liar. I will not listen to his accusations.

- I gird up my loins of my mind. I am cleansed in the Blood. No weapon formed against me shall prosper, and I shall condemn every tongue rising against me in judgment. I am accepted in the beloved. If God be for me, who can be against me?

- My mind is being renewed by the Word of God. I pull down strongholds; I cast down imaginations; I bring every thought captive to the obedience of Christ.

- As the Father loves Jesus, so Jesus loves me. I'm the righteousness of God in Christ. I'm not slave of sin; I am a slave of God and a slave of righteousness. I continue in His Word; I know the truth and I practice it, so the truth sets me free.

- Because the Son sets me free, I am free indeed. He who is born of God keeps me, therefore the evil one does not touch me. I've been delivered out of the kingdom of darkness. I am now part of the Kingdom of Light, the Kingdom of God. I don't serve sin any longer. Sin has no dominion over me.

- I will not believe the enemy's lies. He will not intimidate me. He is a liar and the father of lies. Satan is defeated. For this purpose, the Son of God came into this world – to destroy the works of the devil. No longer will he oppress me. Surely, oppression makes a wise person mad. I will get mad at the devil. I defeat him by the Blood of the Lamb, by the word of my testimony as to what He has done for me, not loving my life, even to death.

- I will submit to God. I will resist the devil and he will flee. No temptation will overtake me that is not common to man. God is Faithful and True; He will not let me be tempted beyond my strength, but with the temptation He will also provide the way of escape (Jesus) that I may be able to endure.

- I will stand fast in the liberty with which Christ has made me free. Where the Spirit of the Lord is, there is liberty – not liberty to do what I "want", but freedom to do as I "ought". The law of the Spirit of Life in Christ Jesus has set me free from the law of sin and death.

- Nothing can separate me from the love of God that is in Christ Jesus, my Lord. His Holy Spirit is my guide, comforter, teacher and best friend! Jesus is my Protector, my Deliverer, my Rewarder, my Refuge, my Strong Tower, my Shepherd, my Light, my Life, my Counselor, my Rock, my Freedom! He is everything to me!

- Christ causes me to triumph. I will reign as a king in life through Christ Jesus. As a young man/woman I am strong. The Word of God abides in me, and I have overcome the evil one. I am more than a conqueror through Christ who loves me. I am an overcomer. I am invincible. I can do all things through Christ who strengthens me. Thanks be to God who gives me the victory through Jesus Christ, my Lord!

WISDOM AND GUIDANCE CONFESSIONS

- The Spirit of Truth abides in me and teaches me all things, and He guides me into all truths. Therefore, I confess I have perfect knowledge of every situation and circumstance I come up against, for I have the wisdom of God. (John 16:13; James 1:5)

- I trust in the Lord with all my heart and I do not lean or rely on my own understanding. In all my ways I acknowledge Him, and He directs my path. (Proverbs 3:5-6)

- The Lord will perfect that which concerns me, and fulfill His purpose for me. (Psalm 138:8)

- I let the Word of Christ dwell in me richly in all wisdom. (Colossians 3:16)

- I do follow the Good Shepherd, and I know His voice. The voice of a stranger I will not follow. (John 10:4-5)

- Jesus is made unto me wisdom, righteousness, sanctification, and redemption. Therefore, I confess I have the wisdom of God, and I am the righteousness of God in Christ Jesus. (I Cor. 1:30; II Cor. 5:21)

- I am filled with the knowledge of the Lord's will in all wisdom and spiritual understanding. (Colossians 1:9)

- I am a new creation in Christ. I am His workmanship created in Christ Jesus. Therefore, I have the mind of Christ and the wisdom of God is formed within me. (II Cor. 5:17; Ephesians 2:10; I Cor. 2:16)

- I receive the Spirit of wisdom and revelation in the knowledge of Him, the eyes of my understanding being enlightened. I am not conformed to this world but I am transformed by the renewing of my mind. My mind is renewed by the Word of God. (Ephesians 1:17-18; Romans 12:2)

I AM...

- I am forgiven. (Col. 1:13-14)

- I am saved by grace through faith. (Eph. 2:8)

- I am delivered from the powers of darkness. (Col. 1:13)

- I am led by the Spirit of God. (Rom. 8:14)

- I am kept in safety wherever I go. (Psalm 91:11-12)

- I am getting all my needs met by Jesus. (Phil. 4:19)

- I am casting all my cares on Jesus. (I Peter 5:7)

- I am not anxious or worried about anything. (Phil. 4:6)

- I am strong in the Lord and in the power of His might. (Eph. 6:10)

- I am doing all things through Christ who strengthens me. (Phil. 4:13)

- I am observing and doing the Lord's commandments. (Deut. 28:13)

- I am blessed going in and blessed going out. (Deut. 28:6)

- I am above only and not beneath. (Deut. 28:13)

- I am blessed with all spiritual blessings. (Eph. 1:3)

- I am healed by His stripes. (I Peter 2:24)

- I am more than a conqueror. (Romans 8:37)

- I am an overcomer by the Blood of the Lamb and the word of my testimony. (Rev. 12:11)

- I am not moved by what I see. (II Cor. 4:8-9)

- I am walking by faith and not by sight. (II Cor. 5:7)

- I am daily overcoming the Devil. (I John 4:4)

- I am casting down vain imaginations. (II Cor. 10:4)

- I am bringing every thought into captivity. (II Cor.10:5)

- I am not conformed to this world, but I am being transformed by renewing my mind. (Romans 12:1-2)

- I am blessing the Lord at all times and continually praising the Lord with my mouth. (Psalm 34:1)

- I am a child of God. (Romans 8:16)

PERSONALIZED DAILY PRAYERS

LOVED ONE IN CHRIST:

These passages of scripture from Paul, David, and Isaiah have been personalized for you. They are powerful prayers, by powerful men, to the Most Powerful! As you pray God's Word back to Him, He is pleased, for He has told us to put Him in remembrance of His Word. Do you think He needs to be reminded? Like He forgot? No, we are the ones who need to be reminded. We claim these awesome promises for ourselves. Pray these daily as the Spirit leads you. You will be richly blessed in doing so.

IN THE NAME OF JESUS,

I praise you Lord from my soul. From my inmost being I praise your Holy Name. I praise you Lord from my soul. I will not forget all your benefits – you forgive all my sins and heal all my diseases. You redeemed my life from the pit and crowned me with your love and compassion. You satisfy my desires with good things so that my youth is renewed like an eagle's. Amen. (Psalm 103:1-5)

IN THE NAME OF JESUS,

As I dwell in the shelter of the Most High I will rest in the shadow of the Almighty. I will say of you Lord, "You are my refuge and my fortress. You are my God and I will trust in you." Surely you will save me from the fowler's snare and from the deadly pestilence. You will cover me with your feathers, and under your wings I will find refuge; your faithfulness will be my shield and rampart.

I will not fear the terror of night nor the arrow that flies by day, nor the pestilence that stalks in the darkness, nor the plague that destroys at midday. A thousand may fall at my side, ten thousand by my right hand, but it will not come near me.

I will observe with my eyes and see the punishment of the wicked. I will make the Most High my dwelling – the Lord is my refuge – so that no harm will befall me, no disaster will come near my tent. God, you will command your angels concerning me to guard me in all my ways; they will lift me up in their hands, so that I will not strike my foot against a stone. I will tread upon the lion and the cobra; I will trample the great lion and the serpent.

Lord, you said because I love you, you will rescue me. You will protect me, for I acknowledge your name. I will call upon you and you will answer me; you will be with me in trouble, you will deliver me and honor me. With long life will you satisfy me and show me your salvation. Amen. (Psalm 91)

IN THE NAME OF JESUS,

No weapon forged against me will prevail and I will refute every tongue that accuses me. This is my heritage as a servant of the Lord, and this is my vindication from you. Amen. (Isaiah 54:17)

IN THE NAME OF JESUS,

I keep asking that you, God of my Lord Jesus Christ, my glorious Father, may give me the Spirit of wisdom and revelation that I may know you better. I pray also that the eyes of my heart may be enlightened in order that I may know the hope to which you have called me, the riches of your glorious inheritance in the saints, and your incomparably great power for us who believe. That power is like the working of your mighty strength, which you exerted in Christ when you raised Him from the dead and seated Him at your right hand in heavenly realms, far above all rule and authority, power and dominion, and every title that can be given, not only in the present age but also in the one to come. And you, God, placed all things under His feet and appointed Him to be over everything for the church, which is His body, the fullness of Him who fills everything in every way. Amen. (Ephesians 1:17-23)

IN THE NAME OF JESUS,

I pray that out of your glorious riches you may strengthen me with power through your Spirit in my inner being, so that Christ may dwell in my heart through faith. And I pray that as I am rooted and established in love, I may have power, together with all the saints, to grasp how wide and long and high and deep is the love of Christ, and that I may know this love that surpasses knowledge – that I may be filled to the measure of all your fullness.

Now to you, God, who is able to do immeasurably more than all I ask or imagine, according to your power that is at work within me, to you be glory in the church and in Christ Jesus throughout all generations, forever and ever! Amen. (Ephesians 3:16-21)

IN THE NAME OF JESUS,

This also is my prayer: that my love may abound more and more in knowledge and depth of insight, so that I may be able to discern what is best and may be pure and blameless until the day of Christ, filled with the fruit of righteousness that comes through Jesus Christ – to the glory and praise of you, God. Amen. (Philippians 1:9-11)

IN THE NAME OF JESUS,

I pray that you fill me with the knowledge of your will through all spiritual wisdom and understanding. I pray this in order that I may live a life worthy of the Lord Jesus and please Him in every way: bearing fruit in every good work, growing in the knowledge of you, God, so that I may be strengthened with all power according to your glorious might so that I may have great endurance and patience and joyfully give you thanks. Amen. (Colossians 1:9b-11)

NOTES

NOTES

NOTES

NOTES

NOTES

NOTES